D1573983

4

1914–1918
INDIAN TROOPS IN EUROPE

Santanu Das

Mapin Publishing

First published in India in 2015 by
Mapin Publishing Pvt. Ltd
706 Kaivanna, Panchvati, Ellisbridge, Ahmedabad 380006 INDIA
T: +91 79 40 228228 | F: +91 79 40 228201
E: mapin@mapinpub.com | www.mapinpub.com

First published in English and in French by Éditions Gallimard, Paris
© Éditions Gallimard/Ministère de la Défense-DMPA 2014

All rights reserved under international copyright conventions. No part of this book may be reproduced or transmitted in any form or by any means, electronic or mechanical, including photocopy, recording or any other information storage and retrieval system, without prior permission in writing from the publisher.

ISBN: 978-81-89995-47-8

Partnerships management: Franck Fertille
Editorial management: Manuele Destors
Editorial assistance: Geneviève de La Bretesche
Art direction: Anne Lagarrigue
Jacket design: Alain Gouessant
Typsetting: Vincent Lever
Picture research: Isabelle de Latour
Proofreading: Sarah Kane
Production: David Angliviel and Marie-Agnes Naturel under
the supervision of Christian Delval
Colour separation: Turquoise
Printed in Slovenia by DZS

This publication is produced with the support of Ministère de la Défense-DMPA, Mission du centenaire de la Première Guerre mondiale, Service Historique de la Défense.

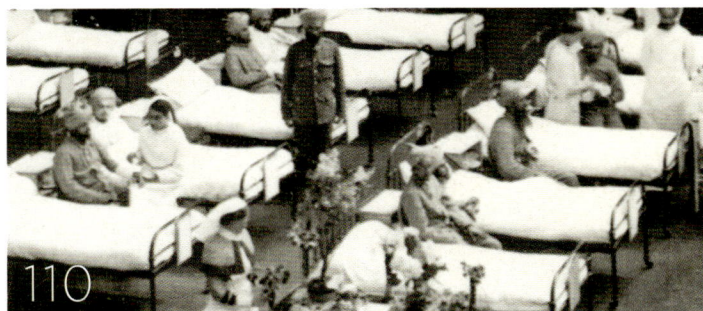

Contents

8 **India, Europe and the First World War**

20 **The home front**

44 **To the front**

60 **The front and beyond**

110 **Hospitals**

128 **Prisoners**

144 **Afterword**

India, Europe and the First World War

'The state of things is indescribable. There is conflagration all around, and you must imagine it to be like a dry forest in a high wind in the hot weather, with abundance of dry grass and straw. No one can extinguish it but God himself – man can do nothing. What more can I write?' wrote Sohan Singh, an Indian soldier of the First World War on 10 July 1915 from the Kitchener Indian Hospital in Brighton.[1] Singh, a sowar or private soldier in the 9th Hodson's Horse, was one of the 138,608 Indians – including 1,923 officers, 87,412 other ranks and 49,273 non-combatants – who served in Europe between August 1914 and December 1919.[2] This book is about these men: it is a visual record of their lives in Europe – in trenches, fields, farms, billets, markets, towns, cities, railway stations, hospitals, prisoner-of-war camps. In the absence of substantial written testimonies, these photographs – though framed by the European gaze – break the silence around them.

Of all the colonies in the British, French and German empires of the time, British India (comprising present-day India, Pakistan, Bangladesh and Burma) contributed the highest number of men. In 1914, it had an estimated 239,561 men in the army and around 20,000 in the Imperial Service Corps. Between August 1914 and December 1919, India recruited for purposes of war 877,068 combatants and 563,369 non-combatants, making a total of 1,440,437; of them, over a million, including 621,224 combatants and 474,789 non-combatants, served overseas between August 1914 and December 1919.[3] These included infantry, artillery and cavalry units as well as sappers, miners and signallers, Labour and Porter Corps, Supply and Transport Corps, medical personnel (particularly the Indian Medical Service) and Remount and Veterinary Services. During the war years, India sent overseas seven expeditionary forces: Indian Expeditionary Force (IEF) A to Europe, IEFs B and C to East Africa, D to Mesopotamia, E and F to Egypt and G to Gallipoli.[4] Between 60,000 and 70,000 of these men were killed. They won 9,200 gallantry awards, including eleven Victoria Crosses (now shared between India six, Pakistan three, Nepal two).[5]

Most of these sepoys (from the Persian word *sipāhi* meaning foot-soldier) were semi-literate or non-literate and did not leave us with the abundance

1 Censor of Indian Mails 1914–1918 (Military Department), India Office Records, British Library, London, L/MIL/5/825/4. The censored mail collection will henceforth be abbreviated as CIM and the India Office Records as IOR.

2 *Statistics of the Military Effort of the British Empire during the Great War 1914–1918* (London, 1920), 777.

3 Ibid.

4 David Omissi, *The Sepoy and the Raj: The Indian Army, 1860–1940* (London, 1994); Rozina Visram, *Asians in Britain* (London, 2002); Gordon Corrigan, *Sepoys in the Trenches* (Staplehurst, 1999); Douglas Gressieux, *Les Troupes indiennes en France 1914–1918* (Stroud, 2007); Franziska Roy, Heike Liebau and Ravi Ahuja (eds), *'When the War Began, We Heard of Several Kings': South Asian Prisoners in World War I Germany* (Delhi, 2011); Gajendra Singh, *The Testimonies of Indian Soldiers and the Two World Wars* (London, 2014); and George Morton-Jack, *The Indian Army on the Western Front* (Cambridge, 2014).

5 See Rana Chhina, 'India and the Great War', http://blogs.icrc.org/new-delhi/2014/04/11/usi-meaworld-war-i-centenary-tribute-project-to-shed-new-light-on-indiasrole.

of letters, memoirs and poems that form the cornerstone of European war memory. Exceptions include the extraordinary, multi-volume wartime 'Diaries' of the Rajput aristocrat Amar Singh, who served in both Europe and Mesopotamia, and the remarkable memoir *Abhi Le Baghdad* (1957) by Sisir Prasad Sarbadhikari. A Bengali middle-class youth, Sarbadhikari served as a stretcher-bearer in the Bengal Ambulance Corps and was held as a prisoner-of-war in Mesopotamia.[6] Unknown works are being freshly unearthed. Memories also persist silently, stubbornly, tangibly. Opening the Gallipoli diary of Private Charles Stinson, 1st Australian Light Horse Brigade, in the Australian War Memorial, one comes across a page where an Indian soldier had signed his name 'Pakkar Singh' in Urdu, Gurmukhi and English; in a small archive in the former French colony of Chandernagore in Bengal, I came across a pair of broken, bloodstained glasses and the photograph of a young man in military uniform wearing them. The label identifies him as 'Dr. J.N. Sen, M.D., M.R.C.S., Private, West Yorkshire Regiment' – he was the only Indian to serve in the Leeds 'Pals' Battalion and was killed in

One of the most popular 'imperial' recruitment posters designed by Arthur Wardle and produced by the Parliamentary Recruiting Committee, 1915.

6 See Santanu Das, *Race, Empire and First World War Writing* (Cambridge, 2013), 70–89, and see Amitav Ghosh's remarkable posts at http://amitavghosh.com/blog/ (accessed September 2014).

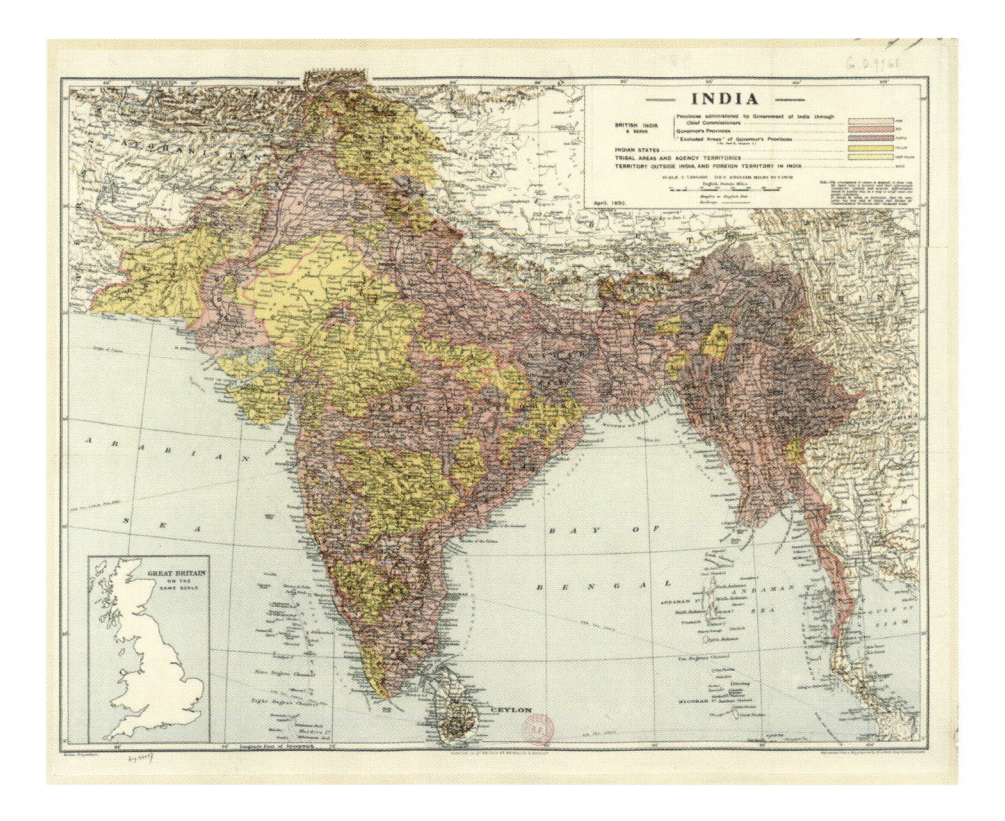

Map of British India: the soldiers were mainly recruited from Northern India (particularly the Punjab), North West Frontier Province and the kingdom of Nepal.

Photographs and medals, including the Military Cross, belonging to Captain Dr Manindranath Das.

A *lota* or brass water-vessel on which a sepoy's name has been inscribed.

7 *India's Contribution to the Great War* (Calcutta, 1923), 156, 161.

8 See Sumit Sarkar, *Modern India, 1885–1947* (Madras, 1983).

France in May 1916. A search through my extended family in Kolkata revealed the war mementos of Captain Dr Manindranath Das: his uniform, whistle, brandy bottle and tiffin-box, as well as the Military Cross he was awarded for tending to his men under perilous circumstances. Das was one among several distinguished doctors from the Indian Medical Service who served in Mesopotamia.

Alongside manpower, the 'jewel in the British crown' contributed its vast resources even as it bled internally. These ranged from minerals (iron, mica and manganese), military hardware and transport equipment to food grains, cotton, jute, wool and hide, to 172,815 animals, including horses, camels and mules. It also made a direct financial commitment. The statute governing India's relationship to Great Britain was amended so that India could 'share in the heavy financial burden'. There was a free lump sum gift of 100 million pounds to 'His Majesty's Government' as a 'special contribution' by India towards expenses of war that was partly raised through war bonds; and in the five years ending 1918–1919, its total net military expenditure, excluding the special contribution and costs of special services, amounted to 121.5 million pounds.[7]

India joined the war as part of the British Empire. The anti-colonial nationalist movement was already burgeoning, particularly in Bengal through the Swadeshi (self-sufficiency) movement (1905–1911),[8] but when the call for the war effort was made, there was enthusiasm across the country. The rulers of the princely states swore loyalty and pledged their resources while the main political parties, including the Indian National Congress and the All India Muslim League, agreed to support. Many of the moderate nationalist leaders, who dominated the Congress at the time, believed that India's war service would later be rewarded with greater political autonomy. Mahatma Gandhi, who was raising an Ambulance Corps in London in 1914, threw himself wholeheartedly into the recruitment drive on his return to India in 1915. He argued that 'we should send our men to France and Mesopotamia. We are not entitled to demand *Swaraj* [self-rule] till we come forward to enlist in the army.'[9] Even Rabindranath Tagore, who had won the Nobel Prize in 1913 and would later decry the war in his powerful lectures on 'nationalism' in Japan and the US, was tempted in 1915 to publish verses supporting the war in *The Times*:

> Now I stand before thee – help me don my armour!
> Let hard blows of trouble strike fire into my life.
> Let my heart beat in pain – beating the drum of victory.[10]

The First World War caught the Indian educated middle-class psyche at a fragile point between a residual loyalty to the empire and a restless nationalist consciousness – very different from the country's position during the Second World War. There were however two important transnational pockets of anti-colonial resistance. The first was the Ghadar party, a diasporic group of Punjabis comprising mainly Sikhs settled in North America: they published powerful anti-colonial tracts and tried to infiltrate the military ranks and encourage armed rebellion. The other was a group of cosmopolitan, nationalist revolutionaries settled

Two sisters selling flags on Flag's Day in London to raise money for the comfort of the Indian Soldiers at the front.

[9] Mahatma Gandhi, *Collected Works* (London, 2006), vol. 15, 3.

[10] 'War Poems from The Times', issued with *The Times*, 9 August 1915, 10.

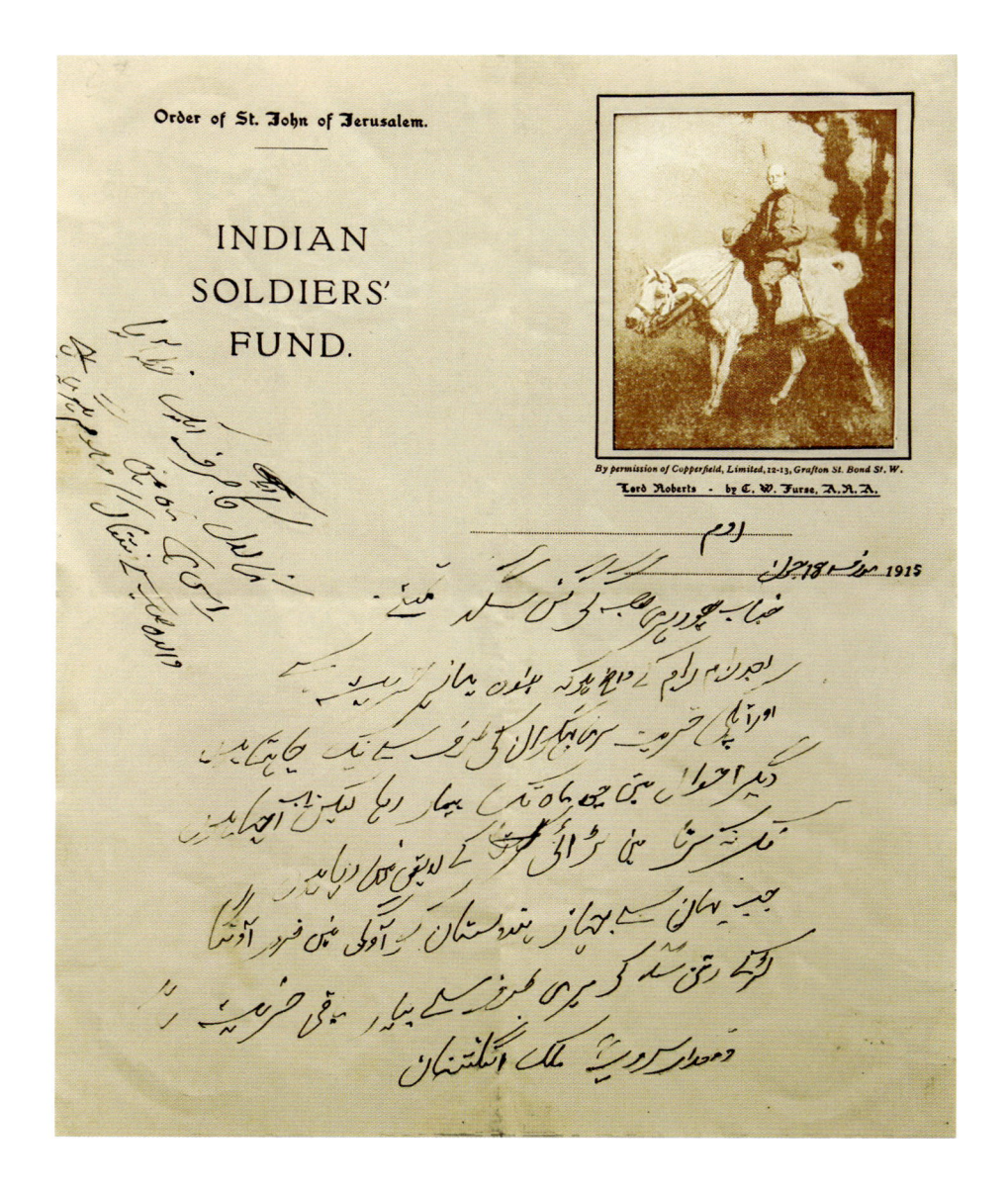

A letter in Urdu and envelope stamped 'Brighton, 16 July 1915' from Sarup Singh to his cousin in the Punjab (Haryana Academy of History and Culture). The letter says he has been unwell but will return to India once a ship becomes available.

abroad who formed the Indian Independence Committee (IIC) in Berlin.[11] But such endeavours were ultimately unsuccessful.

On the other hand, within India, the armed ranks swelled. In 1914, India had the largest voluntary army in the world. But the men were recruited from a narrow geographical and ethnic pool, limited to the peasant-warrior classes in northern and central India, the North-West Frontier Province, as well as the kingdom of Nepal, in accordance with the prevalent theory of 'martial races'. A combination of shrewd political calculation, indigenous notions of caste and imported social Darwinism, it formed the backbone of British army recruitment in India.[12] It deemed that certain ethnic and religious groups – such as Pathans, Dogras, Sikhs, Jats, Garwahlis, Gurkhas – were 'naturally' more war-like than others. These communities were traditionally loyal – often with strong military traditions and low literacy rates – and very different from the politically active and articulate Bengalis who were cast as 'effeminate' and barred from joining the army. Of its almost one and a half million recruits during the war years, the majority came from the Punjab (now spread across India and Pakistan), which saw some of the most intense recruitment campaigns.[13] Why did the men enlist? Financial motives, family and community traditions, social pressures and aspirations, a complex sense of *izzat* (Urdu word for honour) and occasional coercion by the colonial state seem to be combined. The novelist Mulk Raj Anand, coming from a similar military background in the Punjab, notes in his war novel *Across the Black Waters* (1939):

... as the second, third or fourth sons of a peasant family overburdened with debt, they had to go and earn a little ready cash to pay off the interest on the mortgage of the few acres of land, the only thing which stood between the family and its fate. ... Besides, the soldier pledged to fight the battles of the King-Emperor, brought the necessary prestige to keep the policeman at bay and to bail out brothers, fathers, or uncles, who were arrested for non-payment of rent or debt.[14]

Most of these men saw soldiering as a profession and, once the scale of horror became apparent, many sent desperate pleas back home: 'For God's sake don't come, don't come, don't come to this war in Europe.'[15] One wonders how the war news reached the men in the remote rural villages of the Punjab – perhaps sometimes it was the roar of battle conveyed through the letters, and sometimes only a whisper in the fields. As the men left home, the womenfolk sang songs of lament: 'My husband and his two brothers/All have gone to laam [l'arm]/ Hearing the news of war/Leaves of trees got burnt.'[16]

The possibility of employing Indian troops in Europe was raised as early as 4 August 1914 at a war council meeting at 10 Downing Street in London but was shelved. For a 'colour bar' was in force, forbidding the Indian troops to fight the 'white' races for fear it could be fatal, or so the paranoid racist thinking of the time went, to 'white prestige'. In response to the prime minister Herbert Asquith's appeal that all the resources of the 'vast Empire ... shall be thrown into the scale', it was decided that the Indian army would provide garrison troops for Egypt so as to release British soldiers for Europe.[17] But 26 August changed all this: the British Expeditionary Forces, engaged in defensive action at Le Cateau, suffered around 7,800 casualties. A desperate Asquith decided to send the two Indian divisions meant for Egypt to Marseilles. It was a red letter day in the history of the Indian army. Previously, it had fought in a number of 'small wars' along its 500-mile-long north-west frontier, as well as in China and Somaliland. In 1877–78, they were deployed in Cyprus and Malta but not against Europeans and, in the South African War in 1899–1902, they did not have any combatant role. Now, for the first time, they were allowed to fight against Europeans on European soil. If one visited Ypres during the war years, one would also have seen Senegalese *tirailleurs*, North African *spahis*, Maori Pioneer battalions, South African Labour Corps, Vietnamese troops and labourers and Chinese workers. French colonial troops fought on the Western Front. However, of the non-white subjects of the British Empire, only Indians were

Indian soldiers in East Africa being served with quinine as a man goes round with a big bottle.

[11] Maia Ramnath, *Haj to Utopia* (Berkeley, 2011); A.C. Bose, *Indian Revolutionaries Abroad, 1905–1922* (Patna, 1971).

[12] Omissi, *The Sepoy and the Raj*, 1–46; Heather Streets, *Martial Races* (Manchester, 2004).

[13] The Punjab District War Histories, IOR NEG 55540, 5545 and 5547.

[14] Mulk Raj Anand, *Across the Black Waters* (Delhi, 1939; reprinted, 1978), 206.

[15] Havildar Abdul Rahman, 9th Rifles, France to Naik Rajwali Khan, 20 May 1915, CIM, IOR, L/MIL/5/825/4.

[16] Amarjit Chandan in 'How they Suffered: World War One and its Impact on Punjabis', http://apnaorg.com/articles/amarjit/wwi.

[17] See Morton-Jack's careful discussion in *The Indian Army*, 134–139.

Indian soldiers disembark in Mesopotamia with animals and luggage.

18 Much less has been written about the Indian army's non-European experiences: see S.D. Pradhan, *Indian Army in East Africa* (New Delhi, 1990); Radhika Singha, 'Finding Labour from India for the War in Iraq', *Comparative Studies in Society and History* 49 (2007), 412–45; Rana Chhina, 'Their Mercenary Calling: The Indian Army on Gallipoli, 1915,' in A. Ekins, ed., *Gallipoli: A Ridge Too Far* (Wollombi, 2013); and Peter Stanley's forthcoming monograph *Gallipoli: The Indian Story*.

19 *India's Contribution to the Great War*, 97.

20 Nicolas Gardner, 'Sepoys and the Siege of Kut-al-Amara, December 1915–April 1916', *War in History* 11 (2004).

officially allowed to fight. A small number of distinguished Indian pilots also served in the Royal Flying Corps, including the ace Indra Lal Roy who shot down ten enemy aircraft and died in 1918 at the age of nineteen.

Between 1914 and 1918, hundreds of thousands of Indians voyaged across the *kalo pani* or 'black waters' to the heart of whiteness and far beyond – from these fly-infested bushlands of East Africa to the rugged foothills of Gallipoli to the arid tracts of Mesopotamia – to take part in the war.[18] They got an early bitter taste of combat at the badly directed Battle of Tanga in East Africa in November 1914 but soon developed new bush warfare tactics and helped to capture Kilimanjaro Hill in 1916 with British and South African units. In Gallipoli, they acquired new trench warfare skills as they fought alongside Australian and New Zealand forces. One of the final engagements was in September 1918 in the Battle of Haifa when the 15th Imperial Service Cavalry Brigade finally saw mounted action and took part in capturing Haifa and Acre. Indian troops also served in East and West Persia, Palestine, Egypt, Salonika, Aden, Tsingtao and Trans-Caspia. Indeed, to follow the fortunes of the Indian sepoy during the First World War is to trace its global course. The imperial war opened up the world of travel and encounters for these poor peasant-warriors: in Egypt, they went to see the pyramids; in Gallipoli, they shared chapattis with the Australians; in Macedonia, they exchanged coins with Greek labourers; and in Mesopotamia, a North Indian sweeper named Jumman even adopted a recently orphaned Armenian boy found crying near a well and called him Babulal.

Of all the battle-zones, Mesopotamia was India's main theatre of war: some 588,717 Indians, including 295,565 combatants and 293,152 non-combatants (often forming porter and labour corps) – served there.[19] The Mesopotamia campaign has been called the 'bastard war' for its general mismanagement by the India Office and the scandalous lack of medical facilities. After a long, terrible siege at Kut-al-Amara (August 1915–April 1916) during which many Indians starved – some sepoys famously refusing to eat horse-meat – General Charles Townshend finally surrendered; Kut fell on 29 April 1916.[20] Around 10,000 Indians from the 6th Division were captured and brutally treated by their Turkish captors. The debacle at Kut led to widespread criticism. A special inquiry was ordered: the control of the campaign was handed over to the War Office, and Asquith appointed two new British officers, Charles Monro and Stanley Maude. Under their guidance, IEF D was transformed, and, after a carefully planned, sustained advance from December 1916 to February 1917, the Indian troops finally captured Baghdad in March 1917.

The most visible, flamboyant and well-documented troops among the British Indian army however remained the 140,000 who served in Europe. The image of the turbaned and moustachioed Sikh warrior or the lithe Gurkha with *kookri* (fish-shaped knife) in hand, usually with a touch of orientalism (and occasionally self-orientalism), seems to have burnt itself into European cultural memory. From the moment they landed at Marseilles, they seemed to have been chased by the colonial *paparazzi* and subjected to a variety of visual documentation: sketches, cartoons, postcards, watercolours, pastels and even oils. Above all, there are hundreds of photographs, taken by official staff and photographers, amateur enthusiasts and curious onlookers. A photograph, taken in Macedonia, depicts a Serbian showing an Indian officer how to use a camera.

In late September and early October, the first Indian units started to arrive at Marseilles, totalling around 24,000 men. They comprised two infantry divisions – renamed Lahore and Meerut – forming the Indian Corps, and a cavalry brigade. They formed the Indian Expeditionary Force 'A' (IEFA) and were put under the command of Lieutenant-General Sir James Willcocks, one of the most decorated men in the British army. Within a month, the men were in the trenches, straight into the fire of First Ypres. They arrived at a time when, according to Willcocks, 'Ypres was trembling in the balance and each man was worth his weight in gold.'[21] From 23 October to the end of First Ypres, the Indian Corps held around twelve miles or one third of the British line, 'filling a gap in the line when we had no other troops to put in' and helping the BEF to avert a disastrous defeat.[22] Over the course of the next year, the Indian Corps took part in some of the major offensives – Battle of Neuve-Chapelle (10–12 March), Aubers Ridge (9 May), Festubert (15–25 May) and Loos (25 September to mid-October) – and were otherwise mainly engaged in a range of defensive actions.[23] From October onwards, the Lahore and Meerut Divisions were ordered to leave for Egypt and Mesopotamia.

Soldiers wrestling mounted on mules at a sports meeting, Salonika, May 1916.

21 Willcocks's letter to Hardinge, 2 September 1915, Hardinge Papers, Cambridge University Library.

22 Willcocks, 'Indian Army Corps', quoted in Morton-Jack, *The Indian Army*, 148.

23 For a detailed military account of the Indian Corps, see Morton-Jack's monograph *The Indian Army on the Western Front*; also see Corrigan, *Sepoys in the Trenches*; and James Merewether and Frederick Smith, *The Indian Corps in France* (London, 1918).

The Cavalry Corps, on the other hand, stayed on till early 1918 and took part in sporadic offensives, particularly the Battle of the Somme in 1916 and Cambrai in 1917; they did not however get to see any mounted action in Europe.

The performance of the Indian Corps on the Western Front has attracted debate. When leaving, the Indian Corps in 1915, James Willcocks reported to Buckingham Palace that the 'marvel' was 'how much the Indian troops have done and how willingly' while Evelyn Howell, the head censor of the Indian Mail, noted: 'Never since the days of Hannibal, I suppose, has anybody of mercenaries suffered so much and complained so little.'[24] Subsequently, some military historians have questioned their performance, suggesting that they were a group of pre-industrial fighters used to skirmishes on the frontier but inadequate for modern warfare: in the last few, cold, miserable months of 1914, morale plummeted and there was a sizeable number of 'hand-wounds' in the first few weeks.[25] This has been the subject of some debate, and scholars such as George Morton-Jack have recently argued that the Indian Corps became more tactical, battle-hardy and resilient in 1915. Indeed, given how ill-equipped they were in comparison to German firepower and the little training they were given, the Indian Corps did a remarkable job. Casualties continued to be heavy: from January to June 1915, there were around 8,354 men, killed, wounded or missing. There were many accounts not just of exceptional bravery but leadership on the part of the men when their British officers were killed. Of the eleven Victoria Crosses to be given to British India, eight were awarded on the Western Front. While reassessments will continue, it is important to go beyond the simple categories of 'success' and 'failure', or 'hero' and 'coward' – or the equally vexed issue of whether or not, in the absence of hard evidence, they were used merely as cannon-fodder. Instead we should try to understand the wider experiences and emotional tumult of these men in Europe.

For, behind the front line, a whole new world – of travel, adventure, encounters and intimacies – was opening up for these men in which wonder, thrill, excitement, fear, loneliness and trepidation were all fused and confused. The most substantial – and tantalisingly incomplete – sources are the collections of their censored mail, and an excellent selection *Indian Voices of the Great War: Soldiers' Letters, 1914–18* (1999) has been edited by David Omissi.[26] These letters were often dictated by the sepoys and written down by scribes; they were then translated and extracted by colonial censors to assess the 'morale' of the Indian troops, and a selection was forwarded to the chief censor, E.B. Howell. What survive today are these extracts and the covering notes. By early 1915, many soldiers realised that their letters were being read and censored, and they tried to hoodwink the censors. Thus, on 2 April 1915, bugler Mausa Ram wrote from the Kitchener Indian Hospital: 'The black pepper is finished. Now the red pepper is being used, but, occasionally, the black pepper proves useful.'[27] 'Black pepper' and 'red pepper' refer to Indian and European troops respectively, in a coded piece of advice against further recruitment. Neither the transparent envelope of sepoy experience nor just scribal embellishment,

24 Quoted in Morton-Jack, *The Indian Army*, 305.

25 J. Greenhut, 'The Imperial Reserve: The Imperial Corps on the Western Front, 1914–15', *Journal of Imperial and Commonwealth History* 12 (1983), 54–73; Morton-Jack, The Indian Army, 171–86, 220–80.

26 For work on the letters, see Omissi, *The Sepoy and the Raj*; Visram, *Asians in Britain*; and Singh, *The Testimonies of Indian Soldiers*.

27 Mausa Ram from the Kitchener Indian Hospital to Naik Dabi Shahai, 2 April 1915, CIM, IOR, L/MIL/5/825/2, 208.

28 CIM, IOR, L/MIL/5/825/2, 245; L/MIL/5/825/3, 394; L/MIL/5/825/5, 758.

these letters are complex palimpsests where, underneath various accretions, one can hear the echoes of the sepoy heart. Indeed, the Indian sepoy was not a simple *izzat*-driven subject or a naive, hapless victim, but a complex, ambivalent individual, negotiating different cultures, institutions and people.

These letters open up a whole new domain in First World War history and culture, and cover an extraordinary range of topics and emotions, from initial wonder at the agricultural and technological modernity of France ('The country is very fine, well-watered and fertile … Each house is a sample of Paradise'), to the occasional thrilling account of romance and sexual braggadocio ('The ladies are very nice and bestow their favours upon us freely') to the trauma of the trenches. There is a thickening of language as emotions such as horror, resignation or homesickness are often not voiced directly but erupt through images, metaphors and similes:

> The condition of affairs in the war is like leaves falling off a tree, and no empty space remains on the ground. So it is here: the earth is full of dead men and not a vacant spot is left. … [Amar Singh Rawat, 1 April 1915]. Cannons, machine guns, rifles and bombs are going day and night, just like the rains in the month of Sawan. Those who have escaped so far are like the few grains left uncooked in a pot. [Havildar Abdul Rahman, 20 May 1915].
>
> As tired bullocks and bull buffaloes lie down in the month of Bhadon so lies the weary world. Our hearts are breaking, for a year has passed while we have stood to arms without a rest. … We have bound ourselves under the flag and we must give our bodies. [Santa Singh, 18 August 1915].[28]

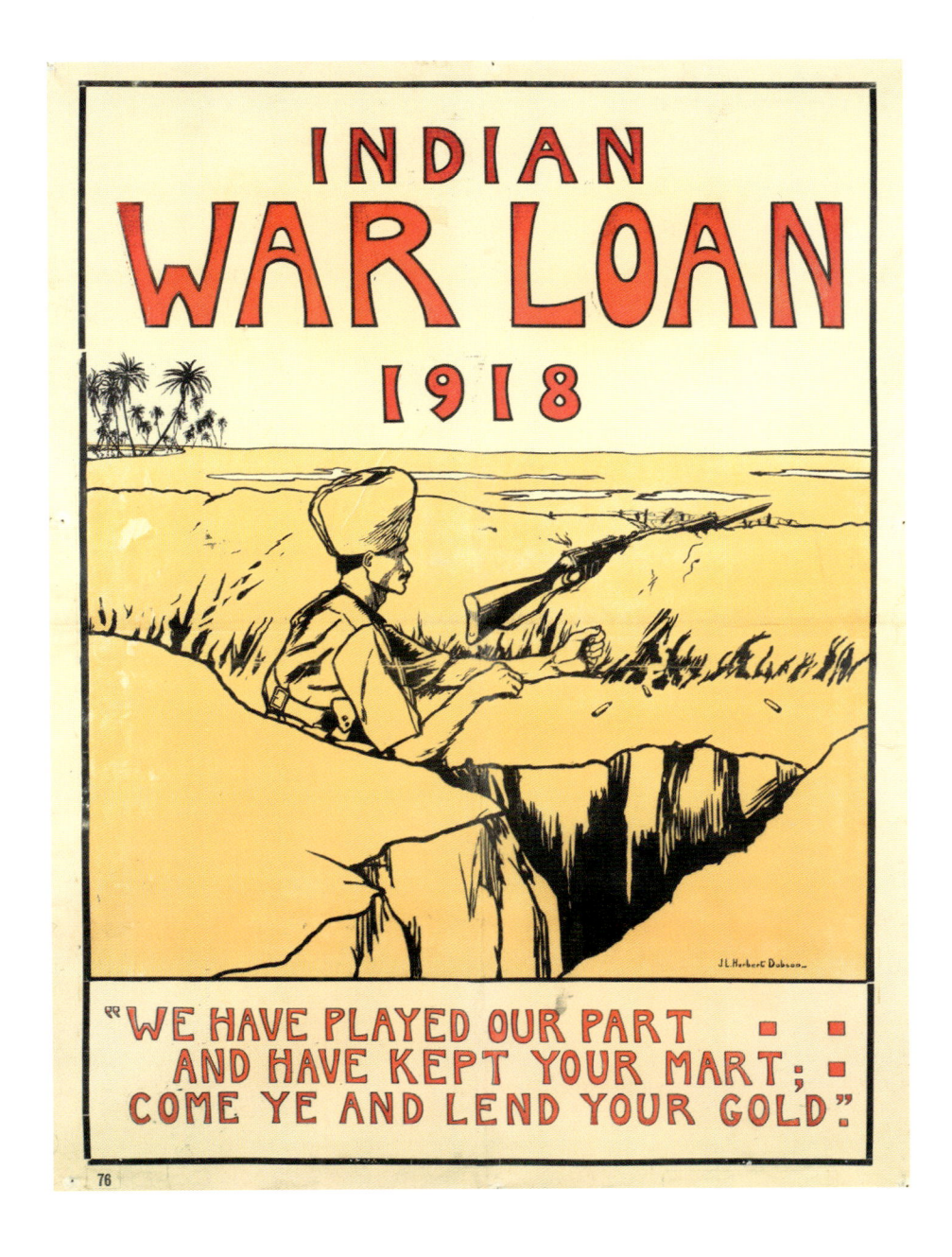

These letters are in many ways the Indian *literature* of the trenches: these men may have been non-literate but being non-literate does not mean being non-literary. One can hear in them the rich

Trenches and palm trees come together in this poster for the Indian War Loan depicting a sepoy with a rifle and scattered bullets.

oral tradition of the Punjab, full of colour, feeling and imagery. Transported thousands of miles from home, they draw on the natural, organic images of the rural communities they had come from to describe the world's first industrial war.

At the same time, France seemed to have created an enduring impression and made them see their own country in a different light, on issues such as gender, education and social equality. A Jat sepoy in France wrote to his family in Jullunder:

> All our eyes have opened since we came to this country. There are no beggars and no poor here. The country produces less than ours. Why then are they so much richer? Because they do not spend money on marriages, funeral and birth ceremonies, &c., and do not put jewellery on their children. The children [in India] go about in ragged torn clothes and yet when they are married we spend thousands of rupees on their marriages. ... What we have to do is educate our children, and if we do not we are fools and our children will be fools also. Give up bad customs and value your girls as much as your boys.[29]

Some of the soldiers seem to have put their observations into practice once they returned to their villages.

But what was the war's impact on Indian institutions and politics? One of the immediate effects was the 'Indianisation' of the British Indian army. If Indian officers, serving as Viceroy's Commissioned Officers, were always subordinate to their British counterparts and not allowed to lead British troops, the post-war years saw the extension of the King's Commissions to the Indian officers. In many ways, it reflected the political mood of the country. For it was during the war years that the nationalist movement in India burgeoned: in 1916, Bal Gangadhar Tilak and Annie Besant formed the Home Rule League and, in 1917–18, Gandhi tried out his strategy of non-violent non-cooperation in Gujarat and Bihar. The nationalist upsurge as well as India's massive war contribution no doubt contributed to Edwin Montagu's declaration in 1917 that 'the gradual development of self-governing institutions with a view to the progressive realization of responsible government' would be the aim of British rule in India.

Yet, as the war ended, promises were broken. The Rowlatt Act of 1919 carried wartime ordinances into peacetime legislation – giving powers to the British to imprison Indians without trial – and infuriated people. Gandhi condemned the 'black' act passed by a 'satanic' government.[30] A watershed moment was 13 April 1919, when the notorious General Dyer opened fire on a peaceful and unarmed crowd of villagers in Jallianwallah Bagh at Amritsar in the Punjab: 379 were killed and 1,200 injured. It is possible that among those killed or injured at Jallianwallah Bagh were First World War veterans who had just risked their lives for the empire. The relations between the First World War and the Indian independence movement are complex and vital, but it is not possible to draw a direct causal connection between the two. The post-war years saw Gandhi's rise to power in national politics, and the Khilafat movement and the nationwide agitations against the Rowlatt Act were very much a legacy of the war. Moreover, the war service abroad inspired fresh confidence and political awareness among the men who came back. As a Punjabi vet-

---

[29] From Risalder, 6th Cavalry, France to Choudhri Jullundur, CIM, IOR, L/MIL/5/827/4, 561 v.

[30] See Sugata Bose and Ayesha Jalal, *Modern South Asia: History, Culture, Political Economy* (Oxford, 2004), 102–19 for further details. The reference to Gandhi can be found on page 110.

[31] Interview with Lance-Naik Khela Singh conducted by Ellinwood and Pradhan, quoted in Pradhan, 'The Sikh Soldier', in *India and World War I*, 224.

eran of the First World War noted in 1972, 'When we saw various peoples and got their views, we started protesting against the inequalities and disparities which the British had created between the white and the black.'[31]

This book is a photographic record of the Indian war experience of both the combatant and the non-combatant. Rather than trying to hold a lopsided periscope on their worldwide peregrinations during the war years, it adjusts its telescopic focus on their life in Europe in intimate detail. It seeks to capture the quotidian fabric of such life – digging, drilling, loading and unloading, marching, road-making, cooking, eating, playing, praying, chatting, resting, mock-wrestling, tending to their horses, smoking an improvised hookah, recovering from wounds or counting days of imprisonment – as framed by European eyes and touched by the shadow of war. The camera had seldom so thrilling or varied a scope within Europe.

Source: *Statistics of the Military Effort of the British Empire during the Great War, 1914-1920* (London: His Majesty's Stationery Office, 1922), 777.

Number sent on World War I service from India up to 31 December 1919

Theatre	Combatants				Non-combatants	Totals		Grand total
	British Officers	British Other Ranks	Indian Officers and Warrant Officers	Indian Other Ranks	Indians	British	Indians	of all ranks (British and Indian)
To France	2,395	18,353	1,923	87,412	49,273	20,748	138,608	
To East Africa	928	4,681	848	33,835	13,021	5,609	47,704	
To Mesopotamia	18,669	166,822	9,514	317,142	348,735	185,491	675,391	
To Egypt	3,188	17,067	2,204	107,742	34,047	20,255	143,993	
To Gallipoli	42	18	90	3,041	1,819	60	4,950	
To Salonica	86	85	132	6,545	3,254	171	9,931	
To Palestine	**	4	4	1	28	4	33	
To Aden	952	7,267	480	19,936	5,786	8,219	26,205	
To Persian Gulf	991	1,059	967	29,408	18,823	2,050	49,198	
	27,251	215,356	16,162	605,062	474,789	242,607	1,096,013	1,338,620
The above figures exclude 42,430 British ranks sent from India to England, all, or nearly all, of whom doubtless proceeded on service from the United Kingdom								42,430
								1,381,050

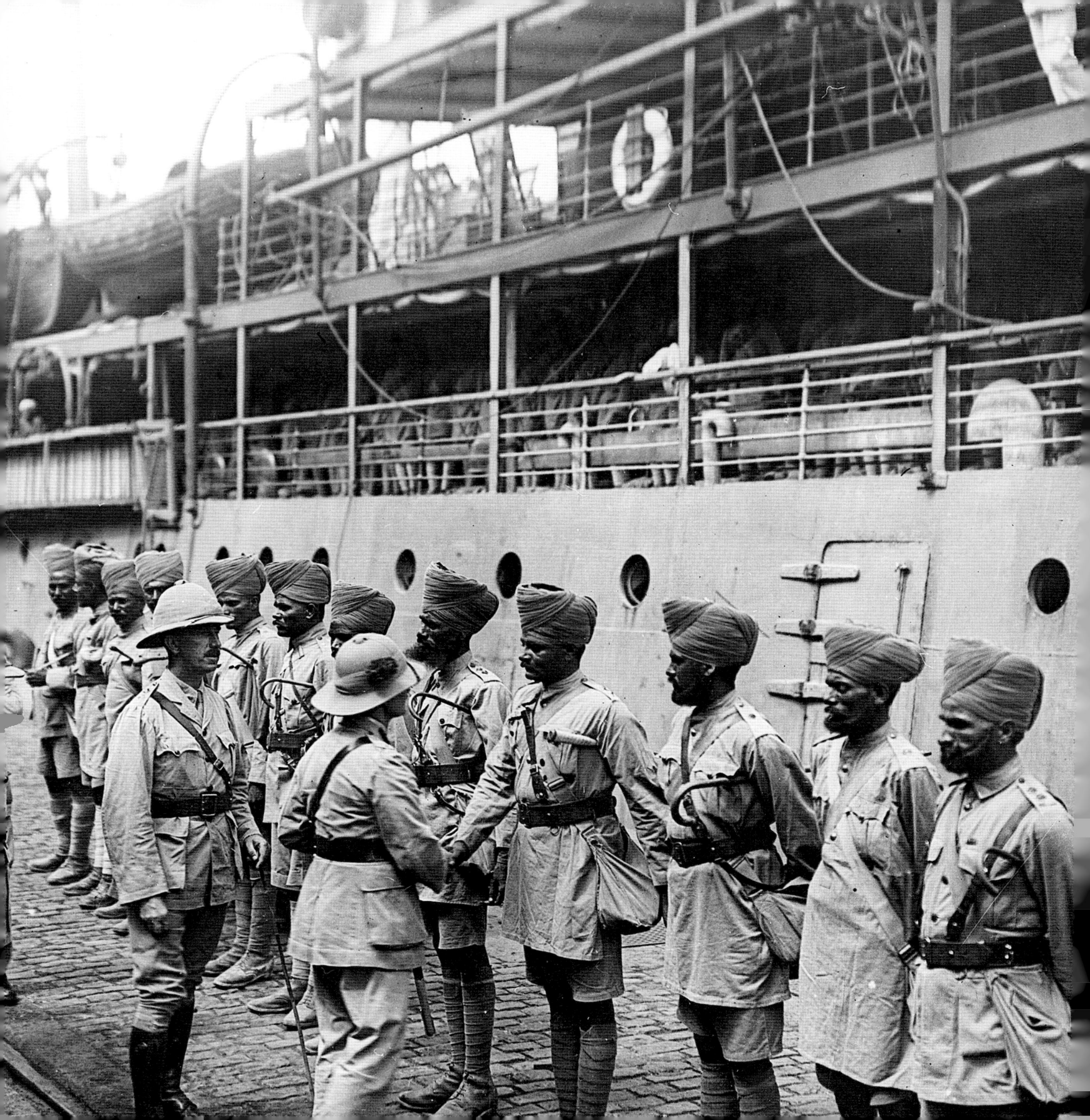

The home front

As Britain declared war on 4 August 1914, Lord Hardinge, the Viceroy of India, announced that India too was at war, without consulting Indian political leaders. Yet, the responses to the war within India, both from the native princes and the political elite, were largely enthusiastic. The two main transnational networks of anti-colonial resistance – the Ghadar party and the Indian Independence Committee in Berlin – had links with the home front but failed to mobilise any large-scale revolutionary uprisings. And barring sporadic food riots, occasional skirmishes and moderate nationalist demands, all seemed relatively quiet on the Indian home front during the war years.

The feudal princes, who still ruled one third of India, were overwhelmingly supportive. They made vast offers of money, troops, labourers, hospital ships, ambulances, motor-cars, flotillas, horses, food and clothes. Kapurthala was one of the first states to pledge its resources while the Maharajah of Bikanir, offering 25,000 men, noted: 'I and my troops are ready to go at once to any place either in Europe or in India or wherever'.[1] The 70-year-old Sir Pertab Singh even vowed to go and sit at the doorstep of the Viceroy unless he was allowed to go and fight! Indeed, the princes vied with each other to serve at the front and on 9 September, when the names of those selected by the Viceroy for service in Europe – the chiefs of Bikanir, Patiala, Coochbehar, Jodhpur, Rutlam and Kishengarh, among others – were announced, it caused a sensation in the House of Commons.

Both the Indian National Congress and the All India Muslim League supported the war effort, though there were some protests against the use of Indian Muslim troops in Mesopotamia. But most nationalist leaders, including Annie Besant who set up the Home Rule League in 1916, backed the Allied effort. India's massive war contribution, these moderate nationalists reasoned, could surely be used to demand greater political autonomy. For Besant, the 'King-Emperor will, as reward for her [India's] glorious defence of the Empire, pin upon her breast the jewelled medal of Self-Government within the Empire'. Mahatma Gandhi however demurred. In his autobiography, he notes: 'I thought that England's need should not be turned into our opportunity', and 'it was more becoming and far-sighted not to press our demands while the war lasted'.[2] In 1917, the Secretary of State for India, Edwin Montagu, declared that 'the progressive realisation of responsible government' would be the goal of British government in India but the 1919 Montagu-Chelmsford reforms fell far short of the country's expectations, including that of the moderates.

Within India, a massive propaganda campaign was launched. Fund-raising was organised, meetings were held in cities such as Calcutta, Delhi, Madras, Bombay, and

'The send-off': British officers bid adieu to the Indian troops.

1 *Speeches of Indian Princes on the World War* (India, 1919).

2 Quoted in G.A. Nateson, *All About the War: India Review War Book* (Madras, 1915); M.K. Gandhi, *An Autobiography; or, The Story of My Experiments with Truth* (Harmondsworth, 1982), 317. See S. Das, 'Imperialism, Nationalism and the First World War in India', in Jennifer Keene and Michael Neiberg, eds, *Finding Common Ground* (Leiden, 2011), 67–86.

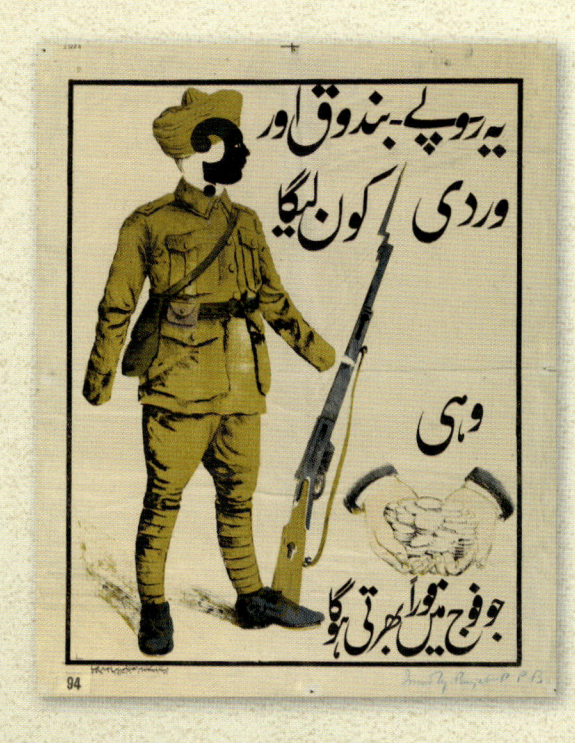

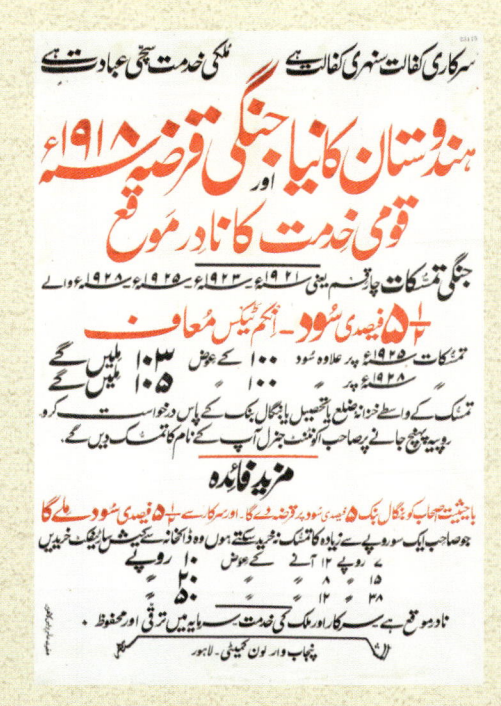

Recruitment poster in Urdu: 'Who will take this uniform, money and rifle? The one who will join the army.'

Poster in Urdu with details of war bonds published by the Punjab War Loan Committee.

3 Sarojini Naidu, 'The Gift of India', in *The Broken Wing: Songs of Love, Death and Destiny 1915–1916* (London, 1917), 5–6.

4 The Punjab District War Histories, IOR NEG 55540, 5545 and 5547. Also see Rajit Mazumder, *The Indian Army and the Making of Punjab* (New Delhi, 2003); and Tan Tai-Yong, *The Garrison State: The Military, Government and Society in Colonial Punjab 1849–1947* (New Delhi, 2005).

5 M.S. Leigh, *The Punjab and the War* (Lahore, 1922), 44.

Lahore, special prayers were offered in mosques; it was said that even Goddess Kali had been enlisted for the Allied cause! Bombay and Karachi were the two cities most physically touched by the war as men, animals and materials flowed through their ports. A literary war journal *The Indian Ink* was produced (1914–16), a recruitment play *Bangali Polton* was written and staged in Calcutta in 1916, and the poet and nationalist leader Sarojini Naidu – 'the Nightingale of India' – read out her poem 'The Gift of India' to the Hyderabad Ladies' War Relief Association in December 1915:

> They lie with pale brows and brave, broken hands.
> They are strewn like blossoms mown down by chance
> On the blood-brown meadows of Flanders and France.[3]

But 1914–18 was also a period of great hardship for ordinary people. There was widespread inflation, and prices of essential commodities – cloth, kerosene oil and food grain – shot up. In 1914, India had the largest voluntary army in the world. As already noted, the sepoys were recruited from a tiny fraction of India's population in accordance with the theory of martial races. Almost half of them came from the Punjab; in districts such as Jhelum and Rwalpindi, 40% of all males of military age enlisted. By 1917, the recruitment base was broadened.[4] By the end of the war, Punjab provided 370,609 combatant recruits, including 190,078 Muslims, 97,016 Sikhs and 83,515 Hindus.[5] The non-combatant labourers, often termed 'followers' – from mule-drivers to *langris* (cooks), *bhistis* (water-carriers) and *mochis* (saddlers) to *dhobis* (washermen) and barbers – came from a different recruitment base.[6]

An intensive recruitment campaign ensued. Trying to lure a largely non-literate population, colonial administrators resorted to posters, speeches, verses and songs. A sepoy or private soldier would get a monthly salary of 11 rupees which was increased to 19 rupees towards the end of the war; in addition, he also got cash rewards, war loans and silver watches.[7] A contemporary poster (see above) – showing an empty military uniform, a rifle and a handful of coins – summed up the threefold attraction of uniform, money and masculinity. Consider the following recruitment song that was composed:

> Here you get old shoes, there you'll get full boots, get enlisted...
> Here you get torn rags, there you'll get suits, get enlisted...
> Here you get dry bread, there you'll get biscuits, get enlisted...
> Here you'll have to struggle, there you'll get salutes, get enlisted...[8]

In 1917, a quota system was introduced whereby each province had to provide a minimum number of combatants, and occasionally coercion was used. In the same year, the Indian government agreed to provide 50,000 labourers for France. The recruitment for the Indian Labour Corps was done so aggressively that it sparked an uprising in the Kuki-Chin tracts in the Assam-Burma border region and in Mayurbhanj, Orissa.[9]

There were domestic pockets of protest too. Women would sometimes trail their freshly recruited men for miles, trying to win them back, and occasionally were even known to throw stones at the recruiters; in the play *Bengal Platoon*, the mother of a new recruit curses the 'red-faced men' – i.e. the British recruiters. In the Punjab, the women often wove their protest and despair into songs:

> War destroys towns and ports, it destroys huts
> I shed tears, come and speak to me
> All birds, all smiles have vanished
> And the boats sunk
> Graves devour our flesh and blood.[10]

In the absence of written records, such songs remain some of the most heartbreaking testimonies and pierce the silence.

In Captain Roly Grimshaw's fictionalised *The Experiences of Ram Singh* (1930), inspired by the eponymous hero's war diary, Ram Singh receives the news of war while on leave in his village in Marwar and travels for four days to reach his cantonment. From their regimental depots, it usually took two weeks for the men to be collected and marched off to railway stations. From 18 August 1914, the men began to arrive at Bombay and Karachi and put up their tents. Here – amidst men, horses, mules, trunks, boxes, ammunition, tears, cheers and trepidation – the ships of IEF'A' would set sail across the *kalo pani* (black waters) with their cargo of human flesh. The rest is history.

A striking version of the colonial visual cliché of Gurkhas with their *kookris* (fish-shaped blades).

6 Radhika Singha, 'Front Lines and Status Lines: Sepoy and "Menial" in the Great War 1916–1920', in K. Bromber, D. Hamza, H. Liebau and K. Lange, eds, *The World in World Wars: Experiences, Perceptions and Perspectives from the South* (Leiden, 2010), 55–106.

7 J. Wilson Johnston, The History of the Great War: Rawalpindi District (Lahore, 1920), 18.

8 'Recruitment song' as extracted in *First World War 1914–1918: Jat Gazette* and translated by Arshdeep Singh.

9 Radhika Singha, 'Indian Labour Corps, 1914–1918', online encyclopaedia.

10 Chandan, 'How they Suffered: World War One and its Impact on Punjabis'.

The picturesque hill-station of Simla was the summer capital of British India, and became the headquarters of many departments of the colonial government during the 'hot season'. Army chiefs, soldiers and officers, administrators and their wives, bachelors and beaus flocked here to escape the heat of the plains or for some summer adventure, giving the place an air of 'frivolity, gossip and intrigue', in Rudyard Kipling's words. The panorama rehearses a typically colonial 'Simla scenario' but here the camera captures the 'natives' looking at two Europeans, while the city with its myriad temples and palaces lies sprawled behind them. In 1913, the city hosted the controversial Simla Accord or Convention, a meeting between the representatives of India, the Republic of China and the Tibetan government to determine the status of Tibet.

The clock-tower at the famous Chandni Chowk in Delhi as a group of curious people, including children, face the camera. The transfer of the capital of British India from Calcutta to Delhi was announced by King George V on 12 December 1911 at the magnificent Coronation Durbar held in Delhi, where he was proclaimed the Emperor of India. A year later, on 23 December 1912, a handmade bomb was hurled at Lord Hardinge of Penshurst, the then Viceroy of India, as he led a grand procession through the city, near Chandni Chowk. He was injured but not killed. The city was formally inaugurated as the capital of British India in 1931.

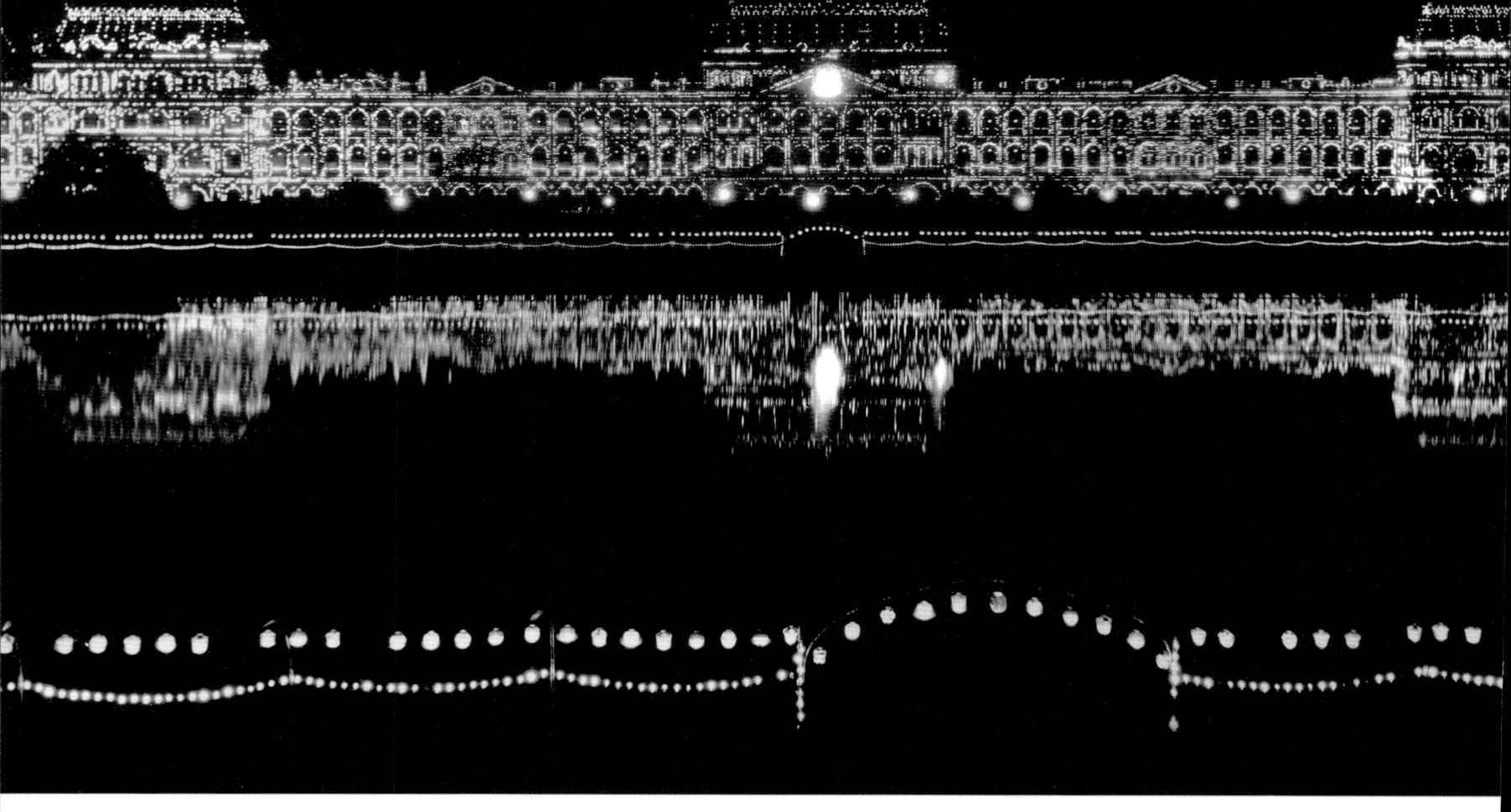

Writers' Building in Calcutta, being reflected on the waters of Lal Dighi (Dalhousie Square or BBD Bag) in front. The serenity of this illuminated and reflected nightscape of Calcutta belies the political turbulence and agitation that rocked the city during the pre-war years. According to Lord Curzon, 'Calcutta is the centre from which the Congress Party is manipulated throughout the whole of Bengal and indeed the whole of India. Its best wire-pullers and its most frothy orators all reside here.' It was the seat of the nationalist Swadeshi (self-sufficiency) movement (1905–1911) which advocated the boycott of foreign goods and saw a number of attacks on the colonial government during the pre-war years.

Bombay (above) and Karachi (below) were the two cities whose streetscapes, sights and sounds actually registered the tumult of the war. Soldiers and non-combatants from all over the country grouped here in order to be shipped off to different theatres of war. At Bombay, the army camped in the city's public parks, overlooked by grand, Victorian buildings, while in Karachi the soldiers camped by the docks or on the racecourse.

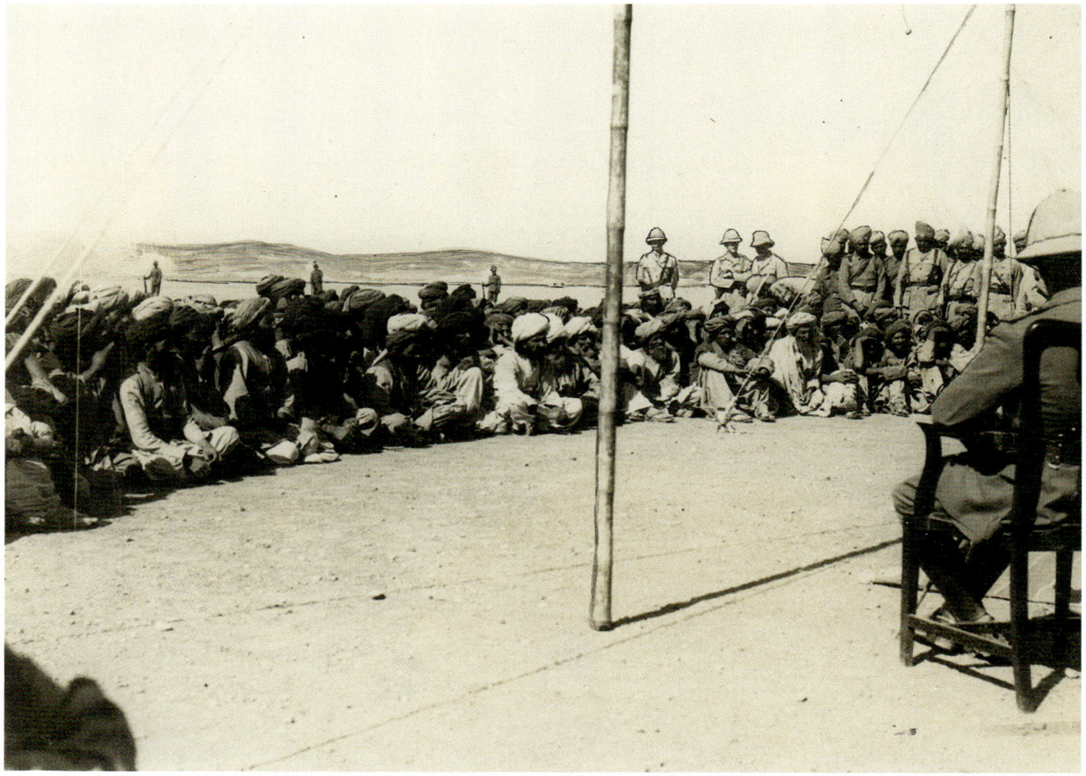

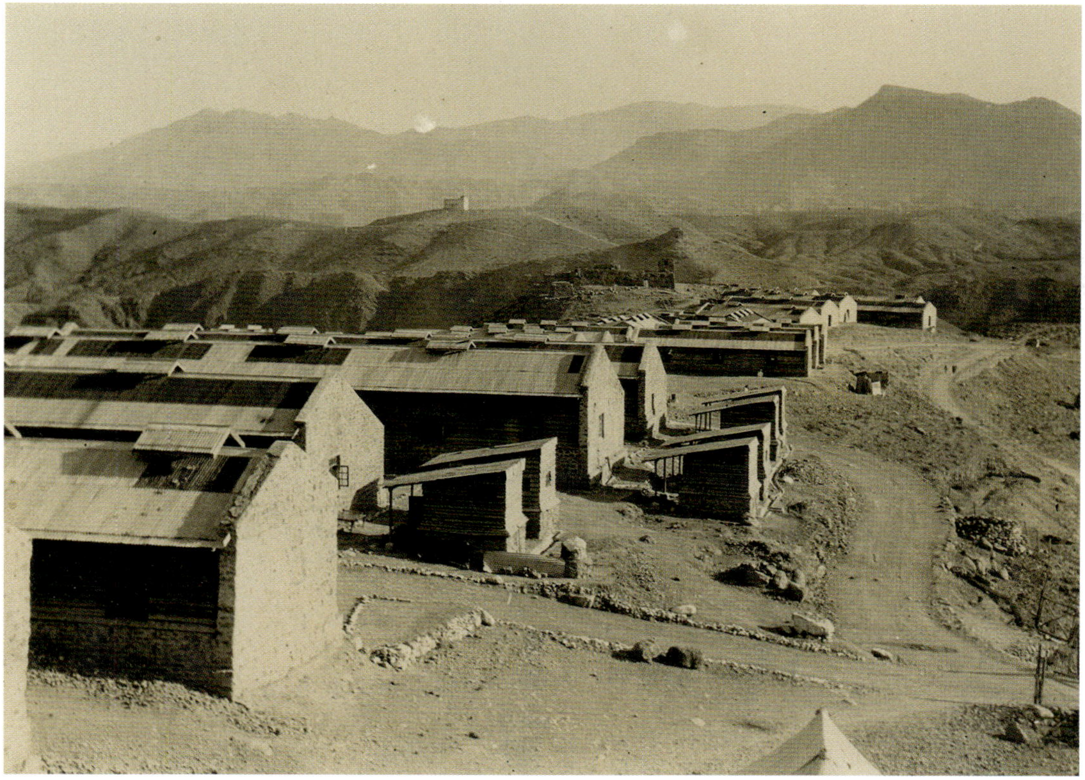

(Above left) A *jirga* (assembly) happening in Dardoni in the North-West Frontier Province where peace terms are being discussed with the Wazir *maliks* (chiefs). Date unknown. (Below left) A view of the quarters of the 54th Sikhs in the barren tracts of the North-West Frontier Province. The buildings were made of metal with corrugated iron roofs that became extremely hot.
(Above) Indian sepoys holding the Emir's troops at bay in the rugged and remote North-West Frontier Province. The region was a running sore on the back of the colonial government in India. Forming the Indo-Afghan border, it stretched for around 500 miles from South Waziristan to the princely state of Chitral. A maze of steep passes, valleys, ravines and pine forests, it was populated by the fiercely independent Pathans of various self-ruling tribes. The area was never fully brought under the control of the British Raj, which waged a number of 'small wars' against these tribes. It did however form an important recruiting ground for the Indian army. The Emir of Afghanistan stayed neutral during the First World War, torn between Britain and Turkey, and the third Anglo-Afghan War erupted in 1919.

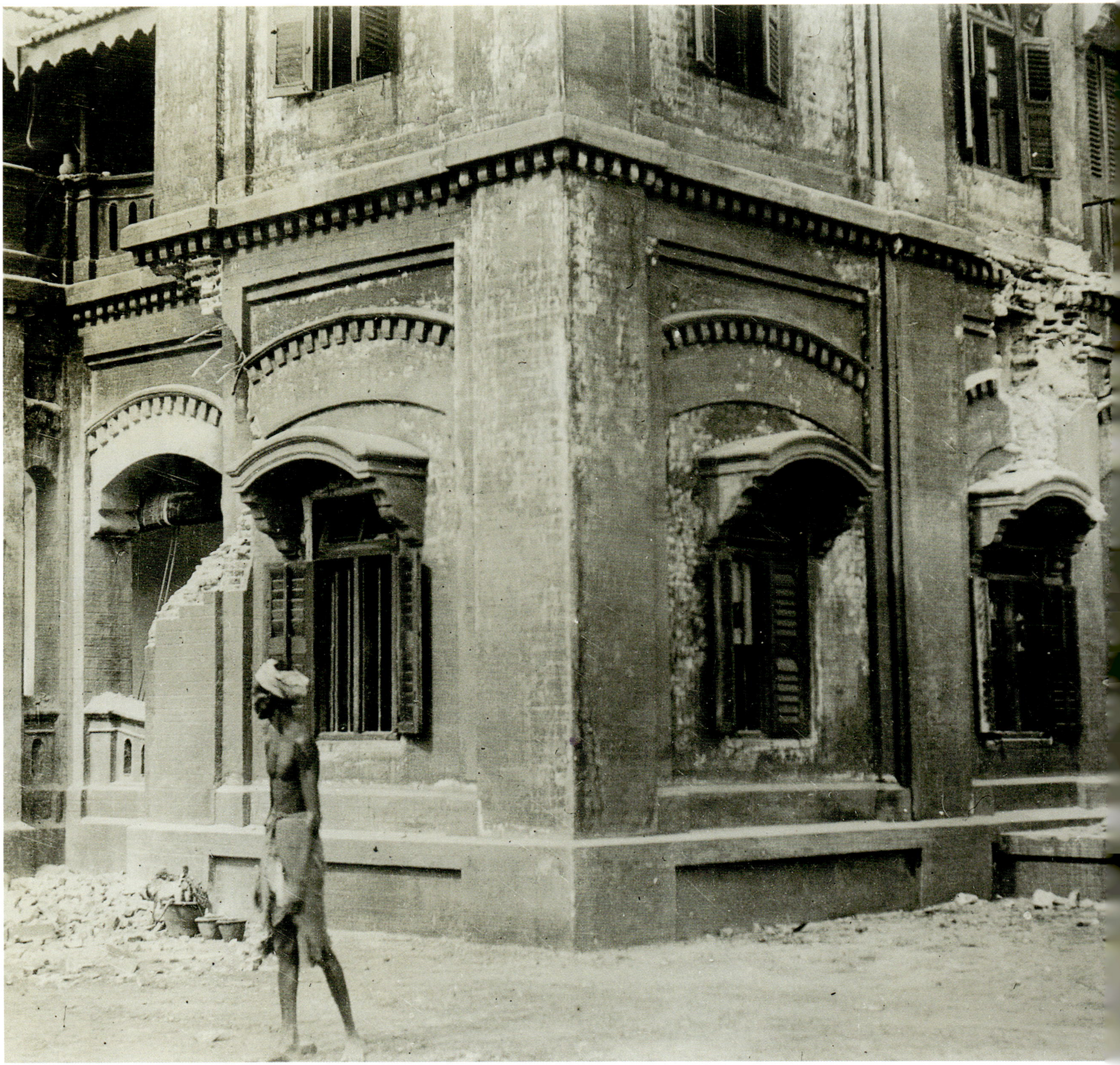

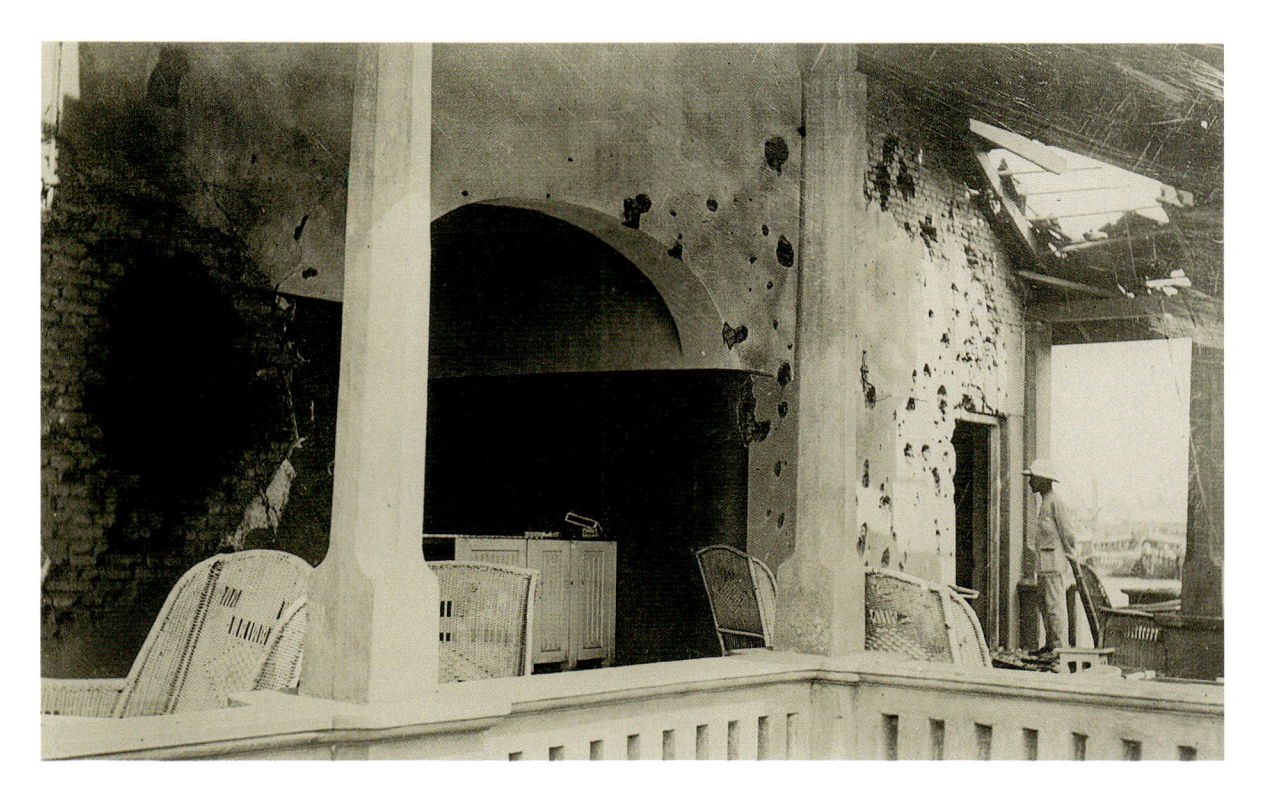

A house in Madras (possibly the Pantheon Club) struck by the German light cruiser SMS *Emden* which spread panic across the Indian Ocean. On 5 September 1914, *Emden* entered the Bay of Bengal, capturing or sinking several vessels, including a Greek collier and an Italian freighter. At 10 o'clock on the night of 22 September, it entered the fully lit Madras harbour and fired some 130 rounds of ammunition, setting fire to two oil tanks, damaging a merchant ship and some buildings. *Emden* received widespread coverage in the Indian media – the object of excitement, panic and rumour. It even made its way into the poetry of the Bengali revolutionary poet Kazi Nazrul Islam (who also underwent training for the First World War) in his famous poem 'Bidrohi' ('The Rebel'): 'I sport with loaded boats/ In my revels/ And send them down to the sea's bottom/ Without mercy.'

(Above) A procession of Indian cavalry through Bangalore. (Below) A party of recruits for the 2nd Lancers at a preliminary musketry drill. The unsure expression on their faces contrasts with the stylised militaristic posture they adopt. The regiment was sent to France as part of the Mhow Cavalry Brigade and was involved in the battles of the Somme and Cambrai. (Right) The European military uniform and accoutrements of the two sepoys contrast with the sandals they seem to be wearing.

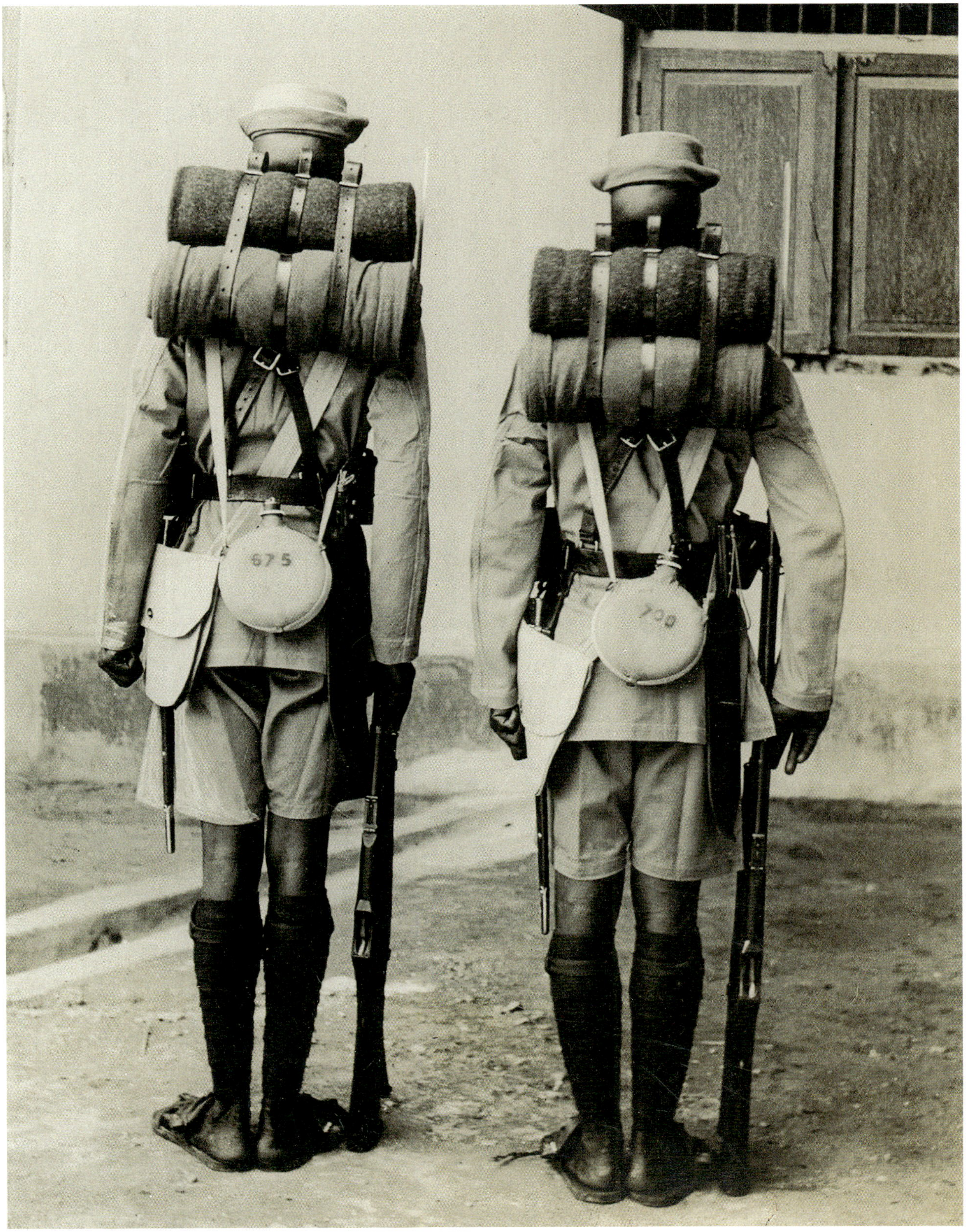

675
700

(Above) A group of Indian women collect the money for the 'Our Day' fund on 19 October 1916 to help soldiers at the front. The group includes the daughter of Maharajah Duleep Singh and well-known suffragette Princess Sophia Duleep Singh and Mrs P. Roy, possibly the mother of the flying ace Indra Lal Roy. (Right) A recruiting meeting is taking place at one of the hill fairs in the lower Himalayas in October 1917. The region was one of the main recruiting grounds for the Dogra Regiment. People sit around or listen to what is possibly a recruitment speech; such lectures were sometimes accompanied by war verses, music and songs in order to encourage and enthuse people to enlist.

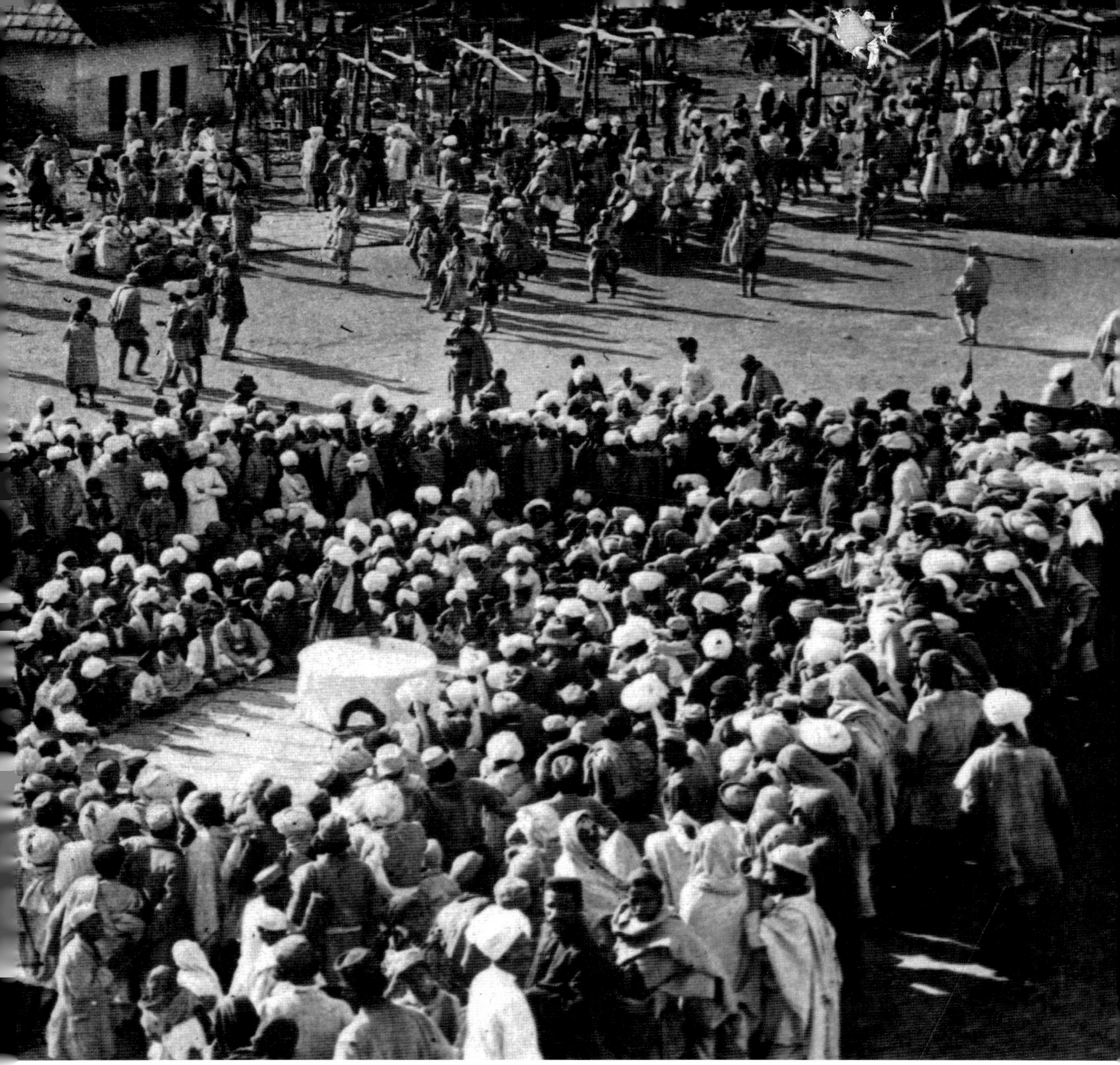

A soldier, unable to write, is giving his thumb-impression on the pay-book. The camera here captures the anonymity of the act as well as the drama of marginalisation, showing not only the economic rudder propelling war recruitment but the story of colonialism itself with its systemic inequalities and power structures. At the time, the Punjab, which contributed more than half the total number of combatants, had a literacy rate of only 5%. Many of the men however knew how to sign their names, and a handful could even write in English.

(Above) A swearing-in ceremony for the infantry taking place in Benares while (below) recruits engage in physical training. A number of training centres were set up across the country, and the daily routine included physical exercise, parades, drills and bayonet-practice.

Home Rule Meeting.
Eager crowds in Madras await the arrival of Bal Gangadhar Tilak, one of the founders of the All India Home Rule League, even as people gather at the Himalayan foothills to recruit or enlist for the imperial cause. Paradoxically, during the war years, the Indian nationalist movement gathered momentum. In 1916, Tilak, along with the fiery Irish theosophist Annie Besant, set up the Home Rule League, and 200 branches were set up across the country. In 1917, the government of Madras interned Besant, causing a nationwide uproar.

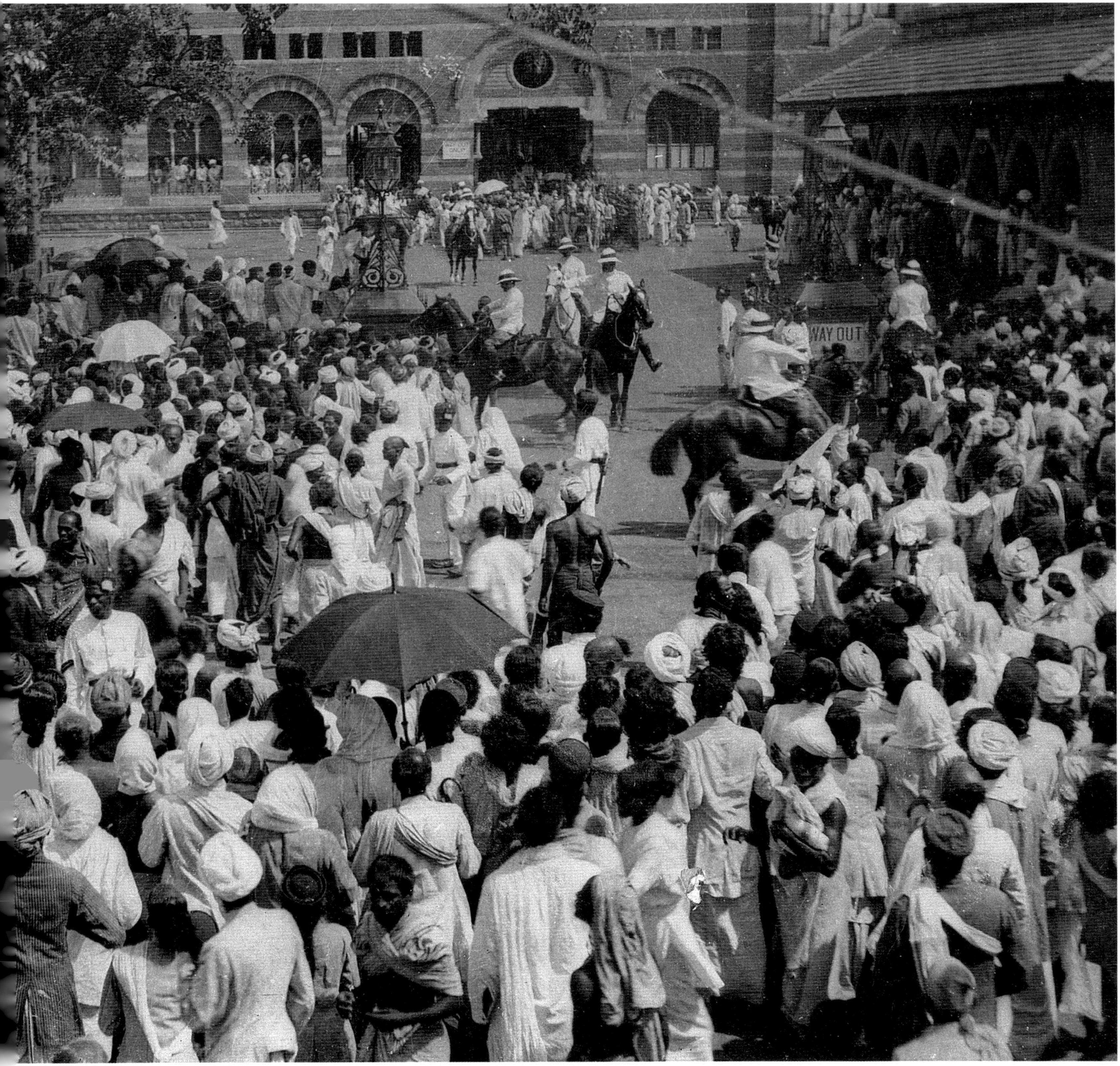
WAY OUT

Mule-carts throng the Bombay docks where the war 'came home' most immediately. During the war years, India sent abroad 172,815 animals, including 85,953 horses and 65,398 mules. Herbert Alexander, 9th Mule Corps, remembered the precarious moment of boarding: 'If by any chance the first mule took exception to the gangway, the probability was that all the rest did the same. Sometimes we had almost to carry them on board. ... There was one animal which had evidently made up its mind that it would not take a sea-voyage ... so some of the men hoisted the beast on their shoulders and bore it triumphantly up the gangway and into the hold: that mule literally smiled over the trouble he was giving.'

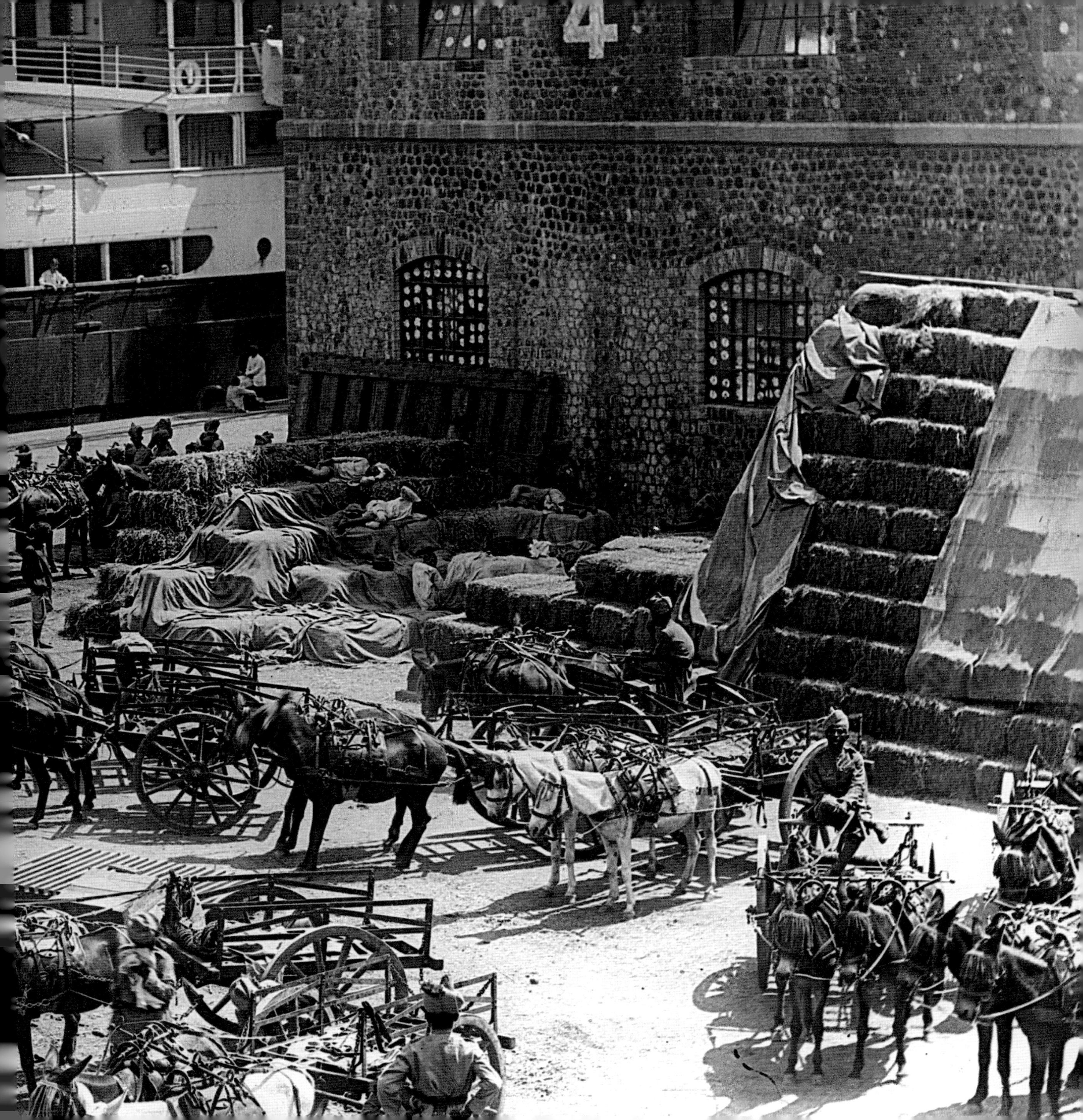
4

(Left) The congestion and chaos as the army loads its material onto the forecastle deck of the ship give way to the neat symmetry of daily drill on the deck a few days later as the instructor is seen ordering the movements (right). In his diaries, Amar Singh, the Rajput aristocrat attached to the Sirhind Brigade, notes the exhilaration of seeing different ships carrying various Indian units cresting the *kalo pani* or 'black waters'.

43

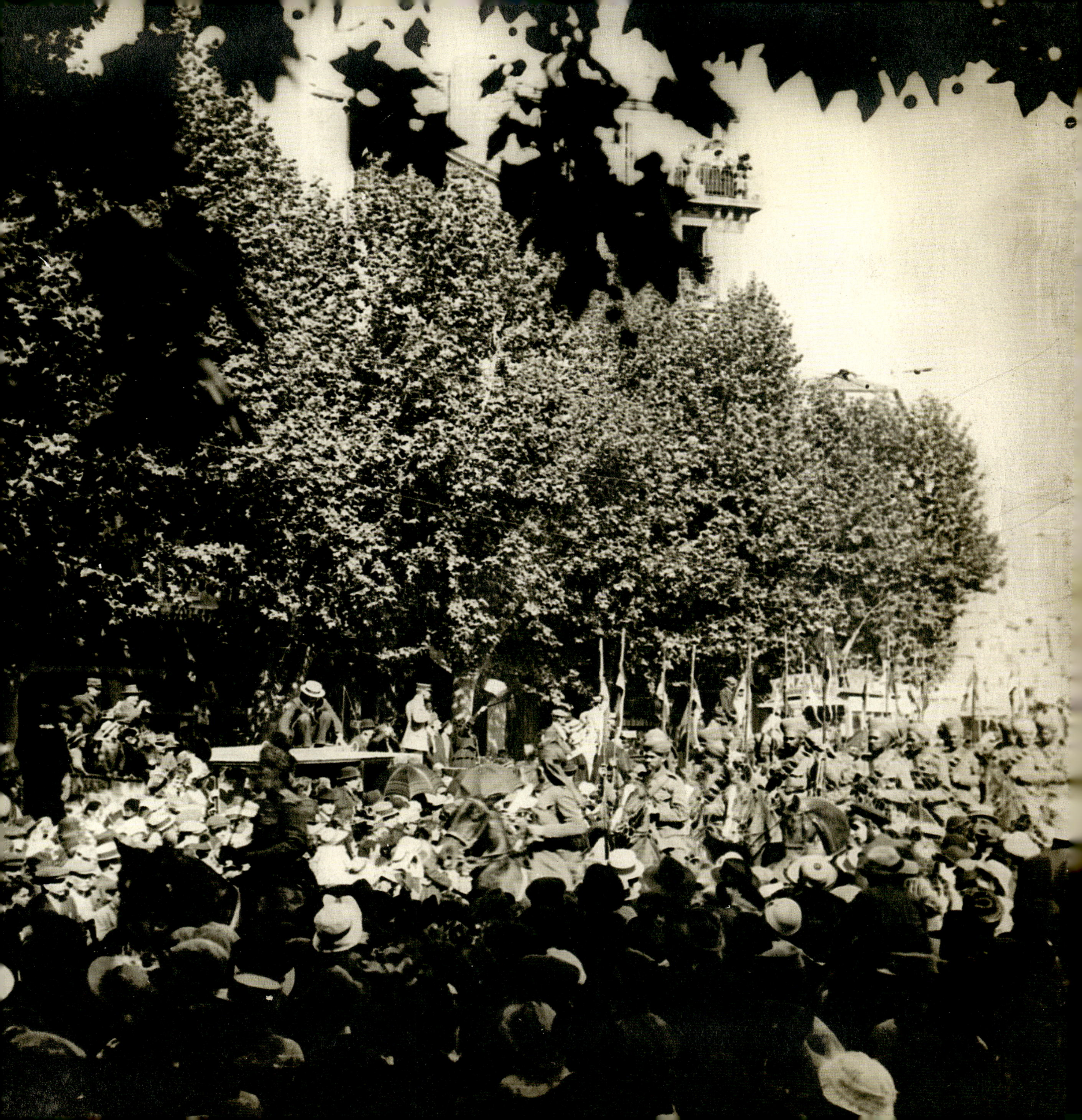

To the front

On the morning of 26 September, amidst autumnal skies and a gentle breeze, the ships carrying the first of the Indian troops from the Lahore Division nudged their way into the harbour at Marseilles. As the anchor was dropped, a group of Indians – bedraggled, seasick but excited – appeared on the deck. The sappers and miners of the 20th Company of the Lahore Division and the 129th Baluchis vied with each other to be the first contingent to set foot on the French soil; in either case, the Indian Expeditionary Force A had arrived.

Excitement exceeded all expectations. Herbert Alexander could not forget the feverish pitch of that morning:

> As the transports passed alongside the many wharves and quays, we could see large crowds collected at every advantageous point to cheer the Indian contingent and welcome it to France. ... As the ships bearing the various detachments came into port, [the 9th Mule Corps] marched off about 9 am. Even at that early hour the streets were alive with people. From docks to camp [we] passed through streets lined with the good folk of Marseilles, who clapped their hands, cheering vociferously and shouting ... At some places we had almost to force our way through the cheering crowds.[1]

'It was a delirious scene', noted Massia Bibikoff, a Russian artist, who soon settled down with her sketch-book to draw the newly-arrived. For her, the Indians charged the war with Oriental romance: 'But I only had eyes for this prince ... The diamonds in his ears, the flash of his eyes, his brilliant smile lent a sort of radiance to his face', she remarked, sketching her princes with their gleaming moustaches and diamond earrings. 'People who were drinking in the cafés of the Cannebière, men, women, officers, stood up on their chairs and shouted, "Vive l'Angleterre! Vivent les Hindous! Vivent les Alliés!" '[2] Women fluttered around the soldiers, clinging, kissing, hysterical; some pinned flowers on their uniforms. During the march, the Gurkhas were apparently mistaken as Japanese!

The soldiers marched for five miles through the beautiful French countryside, warm with autumn colours; they proceeded to Parc Borély and the racecourse where their camp was set up. After unloading their luggage and digging some makeshift ovens in the ground, they made chapattis, attended their prayers and some even tried their hookahs.[3] A similar welcome awaited the Meerut Division on 12 October, though their arrival would be somewhat marred by high winds and sleet. In late October and early November 1914, five more cavalry brigades set sail from India, and by mid-December, they had all reached Marseilles. ' "Marsels!" We have reached Marsels! Hip, hip, hurrah': thus begins Mulk Raj Anand's *Across the Black Waters* (1939), the only

A sea of heads, hats, turbans and lances as rapturous French crowds greet and cheer the Indian cavalry as they parade through Marseilles after their arrival in late September 1914. As the artist Massia Bibikoff noted, it was 'a delirious scene'. Carefully framed by the autumnal foliage, the family grouped around in the balcony high up had possibly the best vantage-point. 'If I were to set about writing down the praises of Marseilles, my hand would be wearied with writing', wrote a sowar or cavalryman from the Sialkot Cavalry Brigade in 1916.

[1] Herbert Alexander, *On Two Fronts, being the Adventures of an Indian Mule Corps in France and Gallipoli* (New York, 1917), 27–29.

[2] Massia Bibikoff, *Our Indians in Marseilles* (London, 1915), 11–12, 114.

[3] See Morton-Jack, *The Indian Army*, 142–3 from which some of the details of the reception have been gathered.

A painting of an Indian lancer by Paul Sarrut, a young French liaison officer with access to the Indian camps, possibly done at Betheune on 16 December 1914.

4 Ibid, 144.
5 Mulk Raj Anand, *Across the Black Waters*, 19.

First World War Indian novel in English, as Lalu the village boy shouts excitedly with his thick Punjabi accent.

At Marseilles, the Indian troops were put under their corps commander, the 57-year-old James Willcocks, who had more battle honours to his credit than almost anyone in the British army. The sepoys' Lee-Enfield Mark II rifles were replaced by Mark IIIs, some of their machine guns with British army Vickers models, and the signals companies' pre-war equipment with more state-of-the-art telegraph apparatus and telephones.[4] Here, they did routine-marches, practised their new rifles and created a little India in foreign fields. Anand, in *Across the Black Waters*, vividly reimagines the scene:

> Habitual early risers, most of the sepoys were hurrying about, unpacking luggage, polishing boots, belts and brass buttons with their spittle, washing their faces, cleaning their teeth with the chewing-sticks which they had brought from home, and gargling with thunderous noises and frightening reverberations, to the tunes of hymns, chants and the names of gods, more profuse and long winded, because the cold air went creeping into their flesh … 'Ohe, where are you going?' Uncle Kirpu shouted. Lalu rushed in, put on his boots quickly, adjusted his turban and walked out again.
>
> 'The boy has gone mad!' exclaimed Kirpu to Dhanoo.[5]

If Siegfried Sassoon in *Memoirs of an Infantry Officer* (1930) had reduced the sepoy to a blob of brown and red, here touch, taste and sound evoke intimately the body of the sepoy and the rhythms of his life, captured beautifully through Anand's long undulating sentence, with its ebb and flow of clauses.

The Indian Corps was moved from Marseilles to Flanders over the next couple of weeks. From the first week of October, the Lahore Division and the Secunderabad Brigade were put on trains to Orléans; they went on a rather circuitous route, heading first westwards along the coast to Béziers, then inland to Toulouse and north to Cahors, reaching Orléans over the second week of October 1914. Here, they got their food: rice or chapatti, *dhal* (lentil soup), vegetables, and meat for those who would have it. A severely limited amount of warm clothing was issued: British war coats, balaclava helmets and warm underpants. The final item was too large for the Gurkhas, and interpreters were sent to the market in Orléans to buy 3,000 safety-pins to make them wearable! Everyone was supposed to be issued with an extra blanket but supply fell short; men of the Wilde's Rifles were spotted wrapped in a variety of fabrics, including tablecloths and curtains.[6] From early November, more clothes would flood in – socks, mufflers, mittens, jumpers – and in December, rubber boots arrived. The Indian Soldiers' Fund Committee was set up to receive donations in order to cater to the needs of the Indian soldiers and labourers.

Orléans was the forward concentration area and supply base. 'The medley of carts of every description that met the eye the first morning at Orléans was enough to turn one's hairs grey', remembered Willcocks, for 'every species of conveyance found a place and the fair at Nijni Novgorod could not have shown greater variety; the char-a-banc and the baker's cart; structures on prehistoric springs; pole and draught harness; horses in hundreds without collars, head or heel ropes – in fact, just loose.'[7] In Anand's novel, Major Peacock deplores the pandemonium in 'twisted Hindustani': "Francisi log acha bandabost nahin" ["The French people's arrangements are not good!"] And he spoke in English: "They know nothing about horses! Look, all the animals running loose. Muddle!". But Lalu, the village boy, watches 'with the open eyes of wonder' only the motor lorries and trucks. 'I would like to see the engine' he says.[8] Meanwhile, his real-life counterpart – a Sikh sepoy – wrote to his uncle in the Punjab: 'No one has a clue to the language of this place. Even the British soldiers do not understand it. They call milk DOLEE and water DOOLO ... [du lait and de l'eau].'[9]

From 17 October, the Lahore Division began to be moved to Flanders to join the British Expeditionary Force. The brief autumnal interlude of the Indian Corps had come to an end.

The portraits of the Sikh and Gurkha soldiers were part of 100 pastel portraits done by Eugene Burnand between 1917 and 1920 and published in *Les Alliés Dans La Guerre Des Nations* (1922).

Sepoys, mules and modern transport jostle together in a frenzy of unloading.

6 Corrigan, *Sepoys in the Trenches*, 46.

7 James Willcocks, *With the Indians in France* (London, 1920), 26.

8 Anand, *Across the Black Waters*, 28, 34.

9 CIM, IOR, L/MIL/5/825.

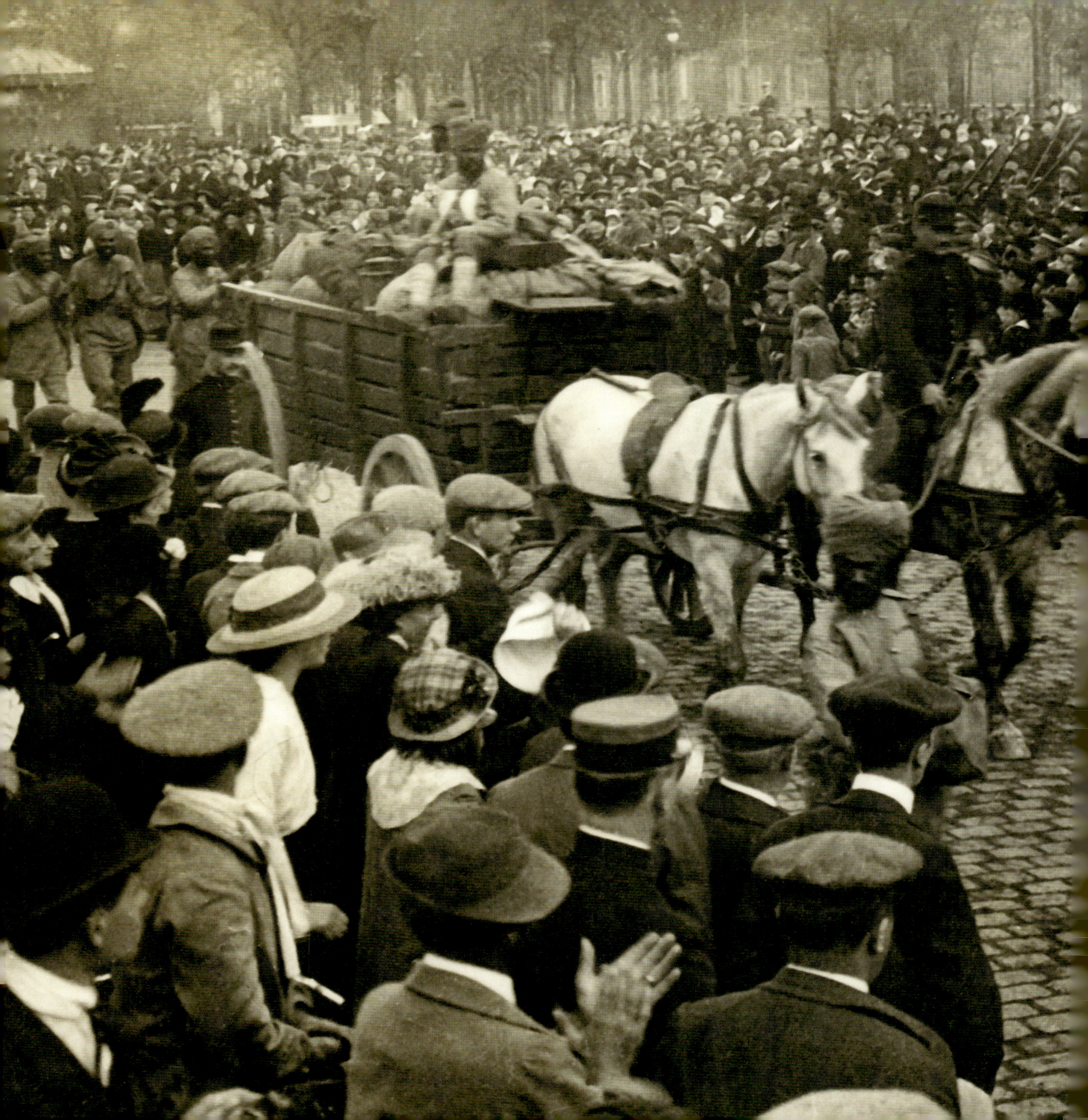

Indian troops march along a cobbled street lined with French civilians cheering their arrival. Some clapped while others chanted 'Vive Angleterre! Vivent les Hindous! Vivent les Alliés'; a few enamoured young women even followed them as far as their camp in Borély. Following the troops were carts laden with supplies. The recently arrived sowars (cavalrymen) with their lances were compared to 'equestrian statues'.

GUERRE 1914. — Au Camp de " l'Indian Army " - Marseille.

The Indian army set up camp at the racecourse at Borély and soon became the cynosure of all eyes. Cameras clicked, photographs circulated, and postcards were printed in thousands. The postcard (above) shows three Indian soldiers in front of a tent with accoutrements heaped all around.

Camp life at Borély: a selection of postcards, showing Sikh and Gurkha sepoys at work and play around their camps, from preparing food and posing for photographs to cleaning and demonstrating their skill with rifles, presumably for the camera.

51

Troupes Hindoues — 7ᵉ Série - Nº 76
Les ablutions rituelles se font pendant un arrêt en Gare - Sourire aux lèvres
Edition historique de l'ancienne photographie Provost, 15, rue Lafayette, Toulouse

La Guerre 1914
Troupes Hindoues — 2ᵉ Série - Nº 81
Le type parfait de l'Hindoue : grand, mince et musclé, remarquable par la régularité et la placidité de ses traits.
Ancienne Photographie Provost, Toulouse

After the Indian troops left Borély they were transported by train to Orléans, via Béziers, Toulouse and Cahors. These two postcards form part of a series of postcards documenting their movement. (Left) Some soldiers washing themselves at a stop-off point on their journey to the front.

(Right) An Indian soldier resting in the doorway of a train carriage destined for Toulouse. This soldier is wearing a winter jumper, which is unusual given the limited amount of winter clothing initially issued to them in Orléans – one of the lucky few!

This official photograph taken in France shows the Indian cavalry on the march with ancillaries. The carts were used to transport tents, water tanks, ammunition, and food such as rice, lentils and flour, while a whole host of non-combatants – from mule-drivers and farriers to *dhobis* (washermen) and *langris* (cooks) – formed an essential part of IEF 'A'. By December 1919, India had sent to France 49,273 non-combatants.

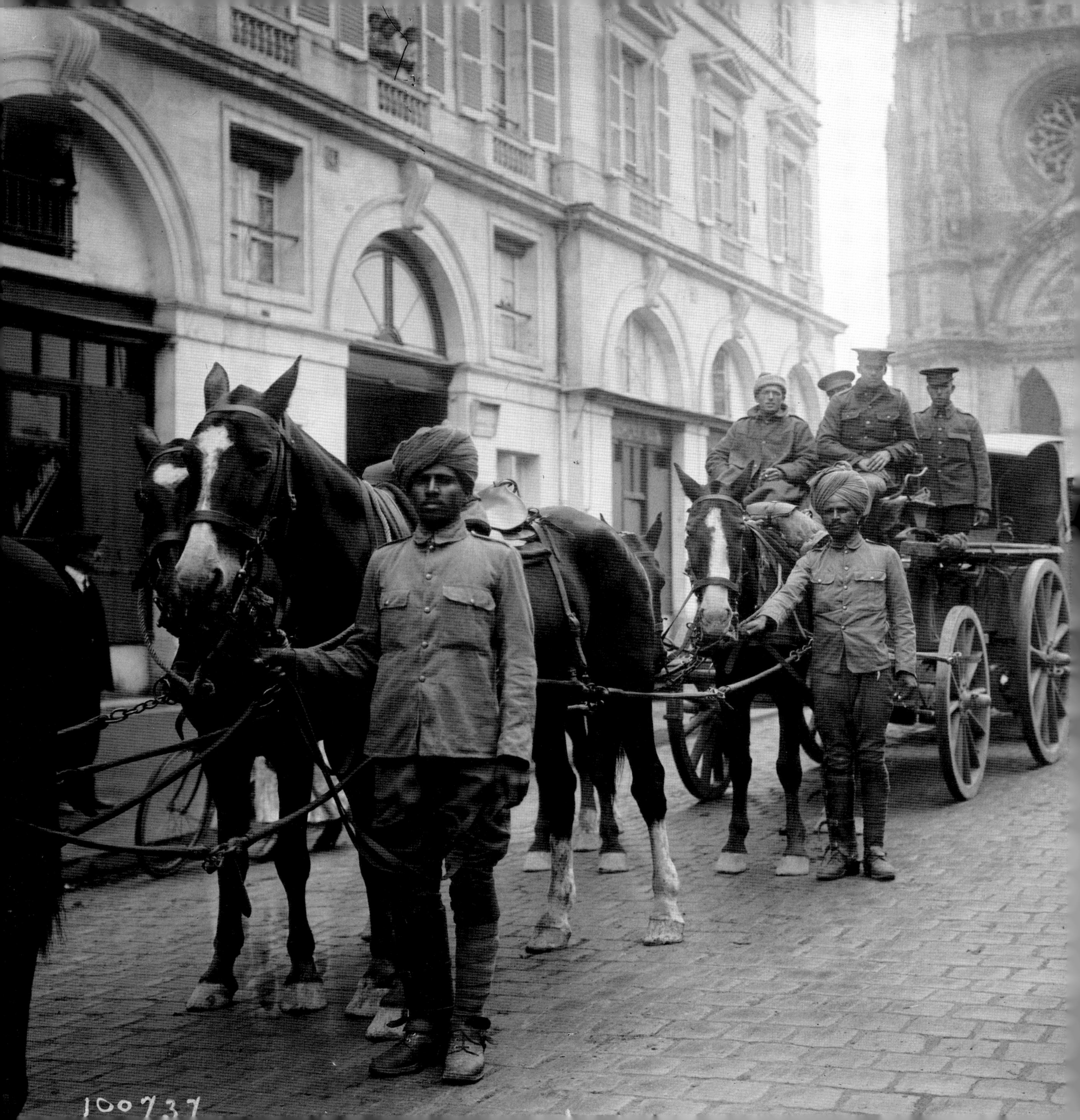
100737

7. AU CAMP DES INDIENS. — On va sacrifier le mouton et la chèvre. 'Pays de France'

1914.. L'Armée Indo Anglaise passant devant la statue de Jeanne d'Arc   British Indian Army passing in front of the statue of yoan of Arc

(Left) Indian and British soldiers outside the cathedral in Orléans: their statuesque postures, perfectly synchronised, match the majestic surroundings.
(Above, top) Another postcard depicting the Indians in camp. One soldier is carrying a sheep while the other soldier leads a goat. After the initial furore over the bully-beef tins, the British army took great care to provide meat according to the religious customs of particular groups.
(Above, bottom) A postcard depicting Indian cavalry and transport carts passing the statue of Joan of Arc in Orléans.

A sepoy wrote of the statue: 'A very fine, handsome young woman. I am looking for them [pictures of her] and have searched many shops. Four hundred years ago that woman gained notable victories in war against the English.'

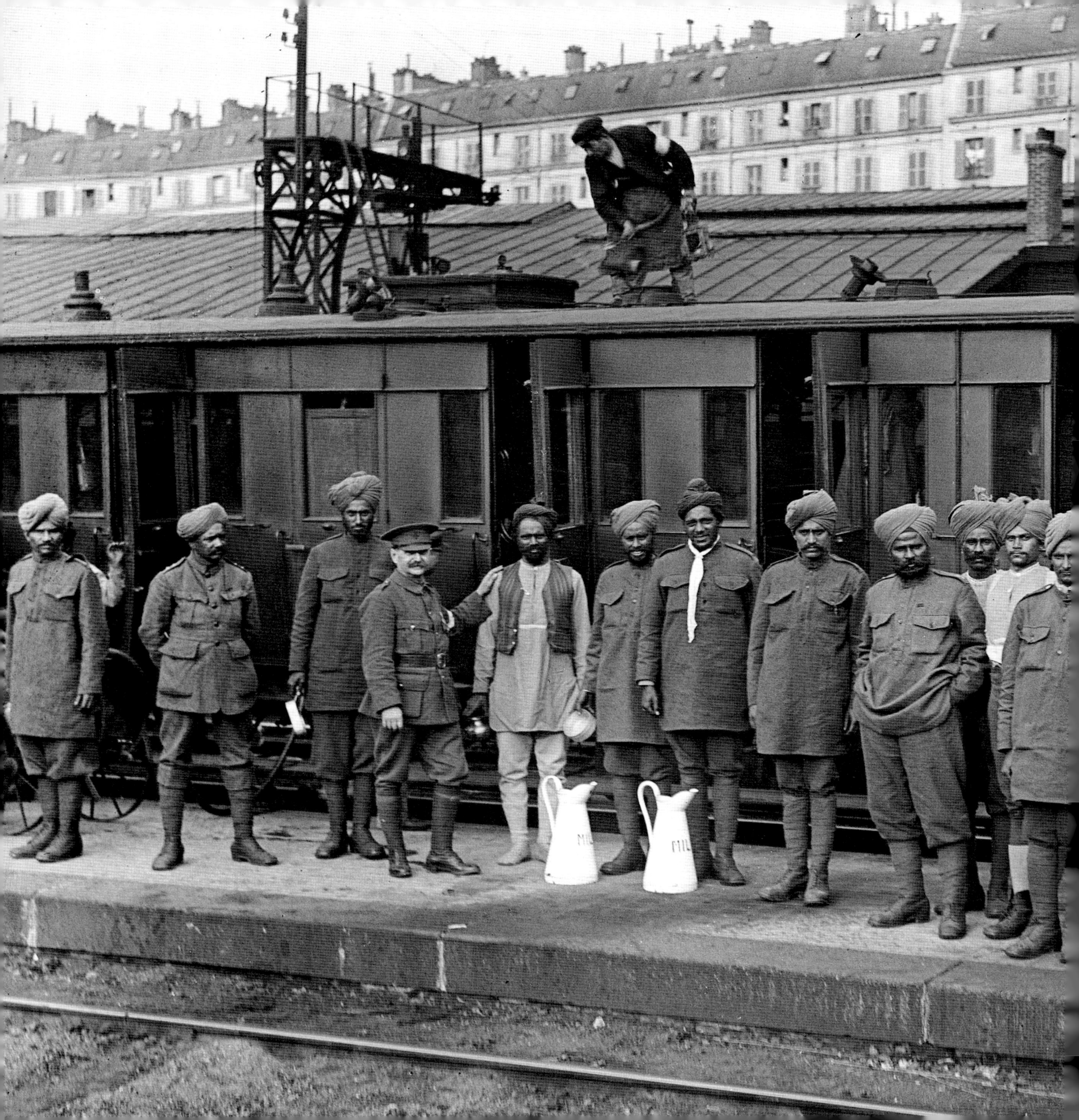
MIL
MIL

A row of soldiers and orderlies just arrived in Paris, against the train and framed by fine Parisian buildings; curiosity seems to have got better of the worker on the roof. The soldiers disembarked at the Gare du Nord in 1915 on the way to the front. In 1916, while changing trains in Paris, a sightseeing tour was organised: the responses were ecstatic. A characteristic letter reads: 'Its [Paris's] beauty is beyond description ... The buildings [and] bazaars are most magnificent and as regards the people they are noted for their beauty. Out of every 100 people, 80 are beautiful, and the remaining 20 are more beautiful than the most beautiful of any other nationality. Moreover, their intelligence and affection and sympathy and politeness are beyond description' (Sirdar Ali Khan, Sialkot Cavalry Brigade, 6 August 1916).

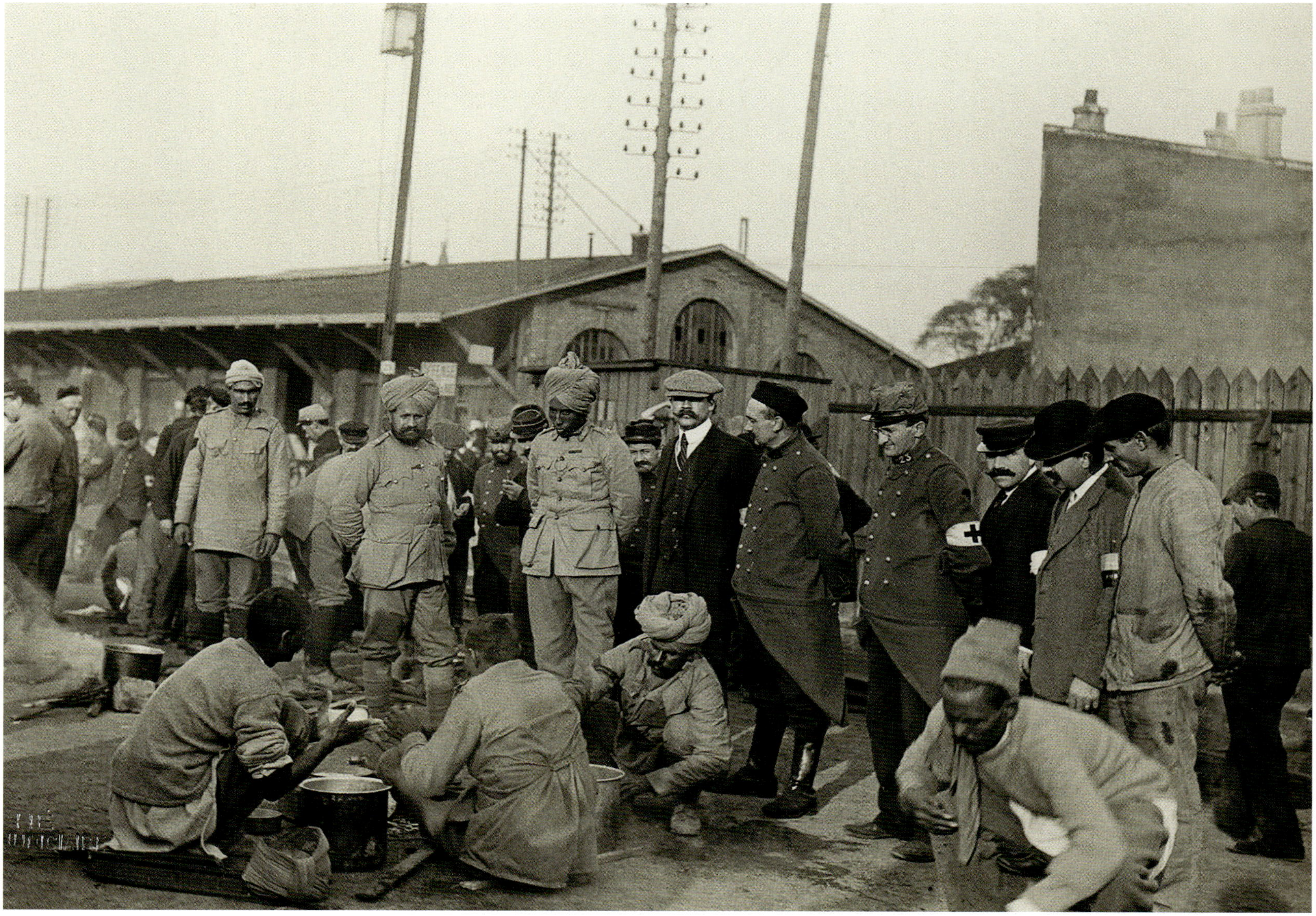

Indian soldiers cooking chapattis at the Gare du Nord (left) while another group make preparations for a meal in Le Landy railway station at Saint-Denis, near Paris, October 1914 (right). Caste and ethnic barriers were already beginning to break down. A cavalryman later wrote: 'When I returned from Marseilles to the firing line, we had to change trains en route, and we wandered about Paris for eight hours. On that day, we all ate at the same table. Our company was composed of five sepoys (of whom three were Sikhs and two Mulims), two sweepers and three cooks; but we all ate together at the same table. Moreover, we have often eaten food and drunk tea prepared by Muslims' (Tara Singh, 6th [?] Cavalry, France, 17 July, 1916).

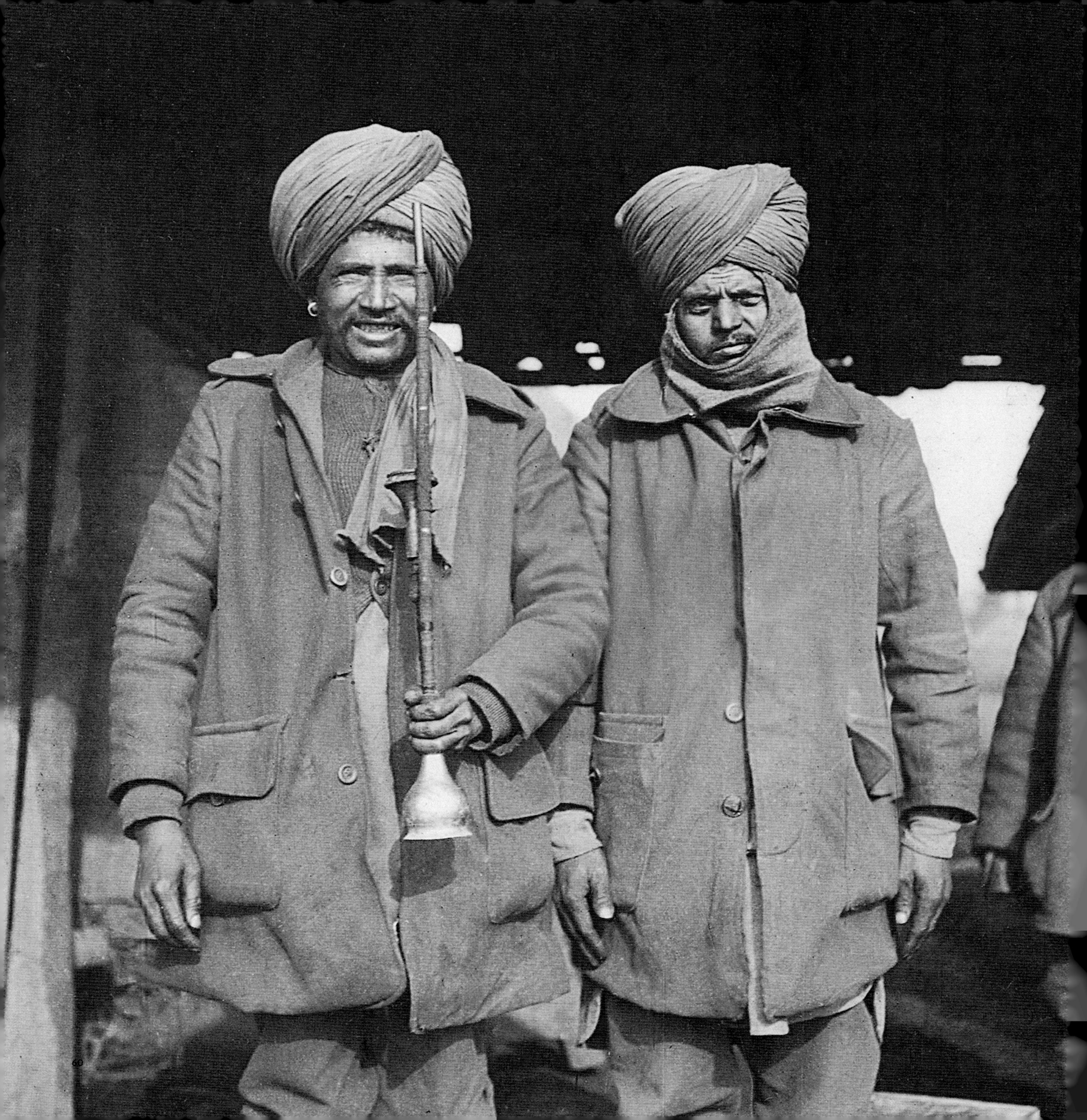

The front and beyond

On 22 October 1914, thirty-six red London buses travelled down an unpaved road, followed by small Indian mule-carts with Punjabi drivers and heaped with ammunition, cooking utensils and other accoutrements. The motley cavalcade was the 57th Wilde's Rifles and the 129th Baluchis on their way to the trenches; by the next day, they were taking part in the First Battle of Ypres (23 October–3 November).[1]

The Indian Expeditionary Force 'A' comprised two infantry divisions (Lahore and Meerut) and six cavalry brigades (Sialkot, Ambala, Lucknow, Mhow, Meerut and Secunderabad). A number of Indian princes and landlords held honorary posts, such as the chiefs of Patiala, Jodhpur and Bikaner. The combatant units were supported by transport, supply, medical and labour units.[2]

The IEF 'A' arrived at a critical time when the British Expeditionary Force was severely overstretched. Douglas Haig reportedly told Sir Walter Lawrence that 'the arrival of [the Indian Corps] saved the situation by filling a gap'.[3] From 23 October to the end of First Ypres in early November, the Indian Corps held around twelve miles or one third of the whole British line and suffered heavy casualties. The initial shock of industrial combat combined with the long, wet winter and homesickness led to fluctuations in morale; there were a sizeable number of hand-wounds, alleged to be self-inflicted. Colonel Bruce Seaton conducted an investigation of 1,000 such 'wounds' and concluded that there was no evidence of self-infliction. However, debates continue among scholars: it seems that in the opening months, many hand-wounds resulted from 'unintentional exposure to enemy fire in the shallow and open front trenches', along with some cases of self-inflicted wounds (as with British, French and German troops in 1914), and two sepoys were shot.[4] Morale picked up in January, and in March 10–13 1915, in the Battle of Neuve-Chapelle, the Indian Corps formed half of the fighting force and held their ground with machine gun and rifle fire. 'Bodies upon bodies and blood flowing. God preserve us, what has come to pass', wrote a sepoy on 18 March while, a week later, on 26 March, a wounded rifleman observed: 'We have been constantly fighting for six months, but we have not seen the sun; day and night the rain has fallen; and the country is so cold that I cannot describe it'. Some sepoys had a conflicted relationship to what they were doing, as did Aamir Khan who stated in his letter that 'our King – God bless him – is going to win and will win soon' but inserted a separate scrap of paper inside the letter saying: 'Our guns have filled the German trenches with dead and made them brim with blood. God grant us grace, for grace is needed. Oh God, we repent! Oh God, we repent!'[5]

Two warmly wrapped men at Neuve-Chapelle. Supplies of winter clothing were initially limited, and many soldiers had to cover themselves with assorted items such as curtains and tablecloths for warmth until new supplies arrived in November 1914.

1 See Corrigan, *Sepoys in the Trenches*, 54–5.

2 See Merewether and France, *The Indian Corps in France*, 10–12.

3 Quoted in Morton-Jack, *The Indian Army*, 153. See Morton-Jack's monograph for investigation of the battles.

4 Bruce Seaton, 'Analysis of 1000 Injuries', IOR, L/MIL/17/5/2402; Morton-Jack, *The Indian Army*, 172 (171–86); Singh, *The Testimonies of Indian Soldiers*.

5 Amir Khan from France, IOR, L/MIL/5/825/2, 141–2; Amar Singh Rawat, IOR, L/MIL/5/825, 184.

THE DAILY MIRROR, JANUARY 26, 1915

THE FIRST INDIAN TO WIN THE VICTORIA CROSS.

This is Sepoy Khudadad, of the 129th Duke of Connaught's Baluchis. He was the first Indian soldier to win the coveted honour of the "V.C." through gallantry on the field of battle. He worked a gun single-handed although wounded. All his comrades were killed.

6.
SIR D. HAIG INTRODUCING ... PERTAB SINGH TO ...
OFFICIAL PHOTOGRAPH CROWN COPYRIGHT RESERVED

Khudadad Khan was awarded the Victoria Cross for continuing to man his machine-gun even after being severely injured on 31 October 1914.

Sir Douglas Haig introducing Sir Pertab Singh, the most flamboyant of the Indian princes, to General Joffre, the French chief of staff.

6 Omissi, 'Europe Through Indian Eyes', *English Historical Review* 496 (April 2007), 386 (371–96); *Visram, Asians in Britain*, 168–9; Claude Markovits, 'Indian Soldiers' Experiences', in Heike Liebau et al., eds, *The World in World Wars* (Brill, 2010).

7 Lance Dafadar Sikandar from France, 12 September 1916, IOR, L/MIL/5/826/7/1129.

8 Sulaiman Khan, France, October 1916, IOR, L/MIL/5/826/8/1272; 16 September 1916, IOR MSS EUR F143/92.

9 Sawan Singh, Rouen, to Sri Ram (Lahore), 24 October 1916, IOR, L/MIL/5/826/8/1338

In 1915, the Indian Corps also took part in the second Battle of Ypres, where they came under gas attack, as well as Aubers Ridge (9 May), Festubert (15–25 May) and Loos (25 September to mid-October); otherwise, they were involved in a variety of defensive actions. Though they failed to secure any substantial ground during these offensives and suffered terrible casualties, their contribution was absolutely vital, and they received high praise from various quarters when they were asked to depart in the autumn of 1915. The first Victoria Cross went to Khudadad Khan who kept manning his machine gun even after being severely injured, while Subedar Mir Dast was the first Indian officer to get it. After the departure of the infantry, the cavalry stayed back and were engaged in a variety of dismounted trench-holding duties. They briefly saw action in the Battle of the Somme in 1916 and at Cambrai in 1917. In 1918, they were sent to Egypt. Meanwhile, the Labour and Porter Corps were employed in a variety of tasks, from loading and forest-clearing to the construction of a British aerodrome in Azelot amidst near-freezing temperatures.

At the same time, behind the front line, a whole range of encounters – from fleeting glimpses of people in towns, fields and markets to sustained relationships with men and women they billeted with – were taking place.[6] Some sepoys picked up French, including the Picard dialect. In November 1915, the Indian Soldiers' Fund supplied 30,000 Hindustani-French phrase books. 'No country is like the country of France', one sepoy opined, while another firmly concluded that, after seeing France, there is 'no need' to see England. France is often compared to 'paradise' and 'fairyland'.[7] There was initially a sense of 'Occidental' ecstasy – 'We have seen things that our eyes never dreamt of seeing' – but, with time, these responses gradually wore off. Everything – from farming methods to manners and gestures to issues such as gender, education and dignity of labour come up for comment: 'In Europe, sweepers, chamars, bhatiyars, Nawabs, Rajas are all one and sympathise with each other … Here labour is not a disgrace, but a glory.'[8] Inaccurate they might have been about European class hierarchies but not insular, as fresh worlds seemed to be opening up in front of their eyes and within their minds. Some men clung on to their beliefs, with one particularly religious soul abstaining from eating with or 'from the hands' of the French. But most reached out, connected and took interest and delight in French life – though, at the end of the day, many felt that they were like 'birds whose nests are in India'.[9]

Some however threw caution to the wind. With time, love blossomed, and as the cavalry moved in 1915 to a new neighbourhood, some soldiers received letters 'of a violently

BATTLE OF NEUVE CHAPELLE 10–12 MARCH, 1915.

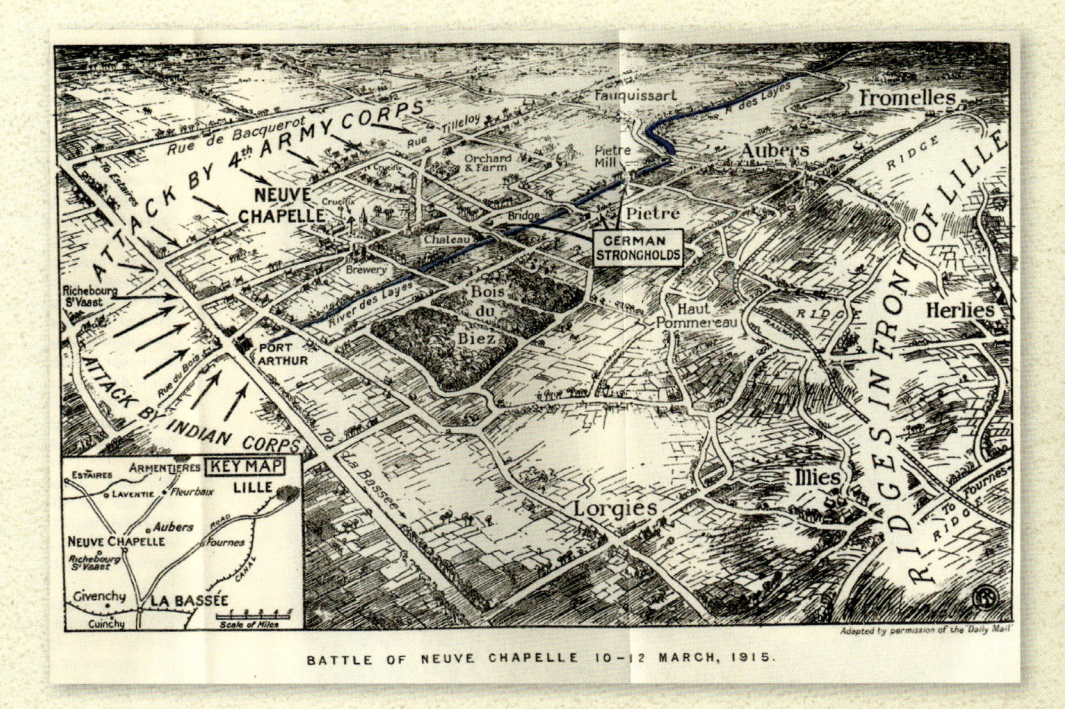

amatory nature' from the French women they had left behind.¹⁰ There were instances of casual sex, but some of the relationships were serious. From late 1916, the British and French authorities would allow the Muslims – though not the Hindus – to marry. Indeed, such a romantic liaison happened in my own extended family. One of my grandmother's cousins, Dr Prasanta Kumar Guha, went as a doctor to France and even got engaged to a French girl. But being a nationalist, he decided to return to India, putting country before love, although they continued to correspond in French. When he later got married in Calcutta, the French lady sent bangles as a gift for the new Bengali bride!

Many billeted with French families, and they recall the kindness and warmth of the local people, 'as if we were their private guests'.¹¹ They were particularly impressed with the hard work French women did in the absence of their men. Some formed deep bonds with their 'French mothers', as evident in the following letter:

> The house in which I was billeted was the house of a well-to-do man, but the only occupant was the lady of advanced years. Her three sons had gone to the war. One had been killed, another had been wounded and was in hospital, and the third was at that time in the trenches. … There are miles of difference between the women of India and the women of this country. During the whole three months I never saw this old lady sitting idle, although she belonged to a high family. Indeed, during the whole three months, she ministered to me to such an extent that I cannot adequately describe her [kindness]. Of her own free will she washed my clothes, arranged my bed, polished my boots for three months. … When we had to leave that village this old lady wept on my shoulder.¹²

Affection, maternity, bereavement, loneliness are all combined. It is not in the world of casual sex and romance but in these affective dyads between the young sepoys and the elderly, bereaved French women that some of the most fruitful Indo-European encounters took place. No wonder, an Indian sepoy wrote, 'after we are gone we shall mostly remember France very kindly'.¹³

A map of Neuve-Chapelle illustrating the directions of the attacks on the Germans from the British and Indian armies during the Battle of Neuve-Chapelle which raged from 10 to 13 March 1915.

A fan-shaped orientalist battle-scene by Italian graphic artist Alberto Fabio Lorenzi depicting Sikhs charging with *kirpans* (daggers) in their mouths.

10 NBC, 21 August 1915, IOR L/MIL/5/825/4/703.

11 2 January 1916, IOR, L/MIL/828/2.

12 Letter of Sher Bahadur Khan, France, 9 January 1916, IOR, L/MIL/5/828/112.

13 IOR MSS EUR F143/89, 5 January 1916.

63

(Left) Indian infantry marching to the front with newly issued Mark III rifles slung over their shoulders and packs containing their equipment. The third sepoy from the right glances to his left and smiles. There was no Indian equivalent of 'Tipperary' to relieve the tedium of the march.

(Right) A famously 'staged' scene: the second line of Gurkhas, rushing in to consolidate a trench taken by the first line, comes under shellfire. In the foreground of the photograph, one can see a British officer directing a group of Gurkhas who are reinforcing a trench they have just taken, while in the background a plume of smoke rises from the trench. This photograph is part of a large collection taken by the Canadian-born photographer H.D. Girdwood. The action shots were staged.

65

Gurkhas digging communication trenches and laying cables to connect up advanced positions.

(Above) A stereoview card depicting Indian men digging and reinforcing the trenches. 'No more hastily dug trenches full of slime and water, but model breastworks', noted General Willcocks as the sepoys dug increasingly sophisticated trenches, giving them names such as 'Baluchi Road' or 'Ludhiana Lane'. But Lieutenant-Colonel J.W. Barnett wrote: 'Don't think it is fair that men should have to dig in open daylight 200 yards from Germans – it is murder really.' (Right) Indian infantry from the 58th Rifles training against gas attacks in the trenches at Fauquissart in France. When Germany first used chlorine gas against Allied troops at Second Ypres in April 1915, British and Indian soldiers were unprotected. The Indian soldiers in this photograph are wearing a rudimentary form of protection called the British Smoke Hood, which was developed by Dr Cluny MacPherson of the Royal Newfoundland Regiment. The hood was made out of fabric that needed saturation in the anti-gas chemical solutions and was fitted with a celluloid window for visibility. A staged stereoview, taken by H.D. Girdwood.

67

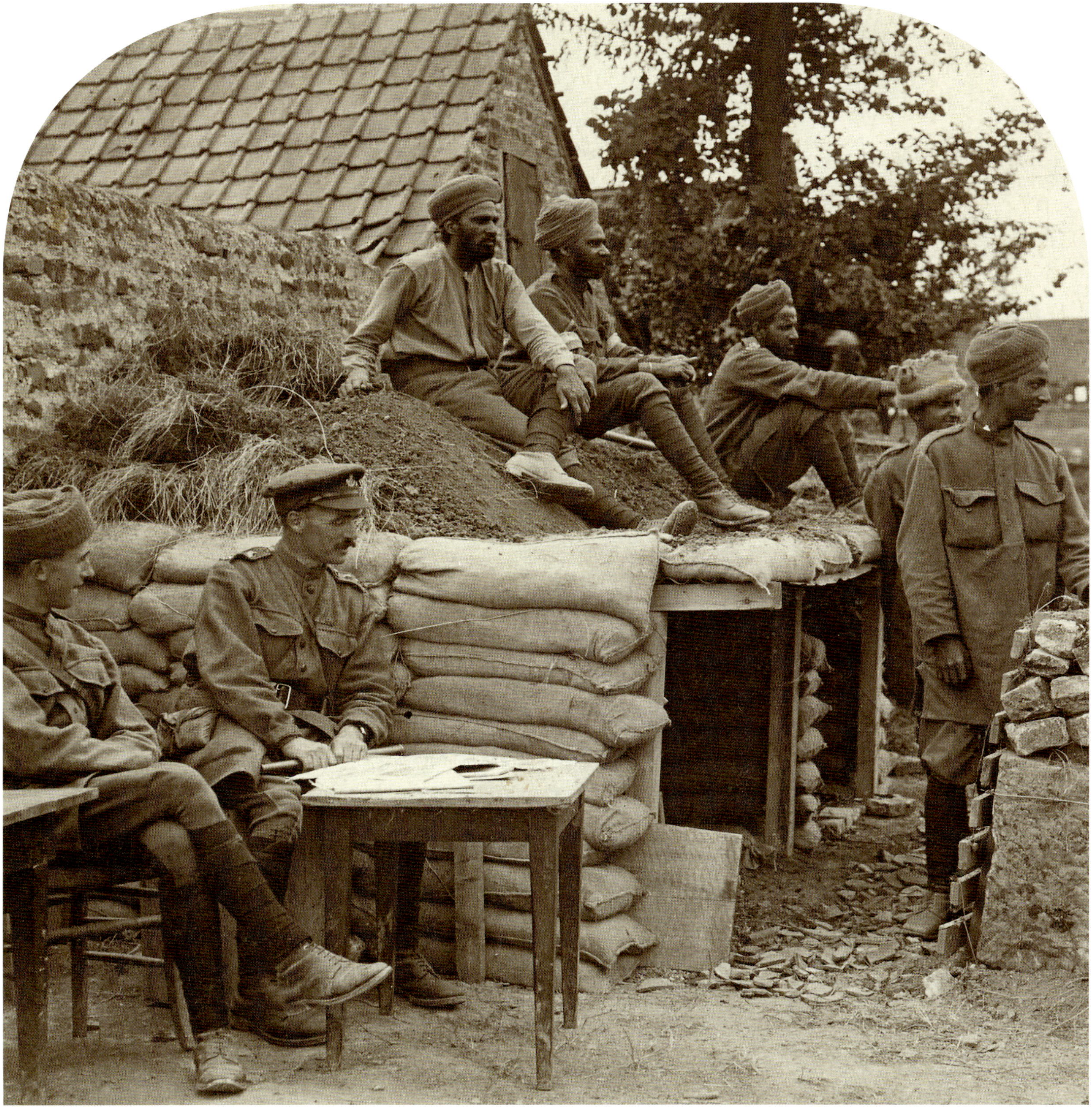

(Left) This photograph, taken by H.D. Girdwood, shows a newly constructed officers' shelter lined with sandbags behind the front line; houses are visible in the background. Along with two British officers on the left, a group of Indian sepoys look ahead, absorbed by what is going on. This image and the one to the right are part of a large collection of stereoscopic images of battle-scenes made during the First World War in Britain, France and Germany.

(Above) Soldiers from the Scottish Black Watch Regiment and 41st Dogras in a trench on 9 August 1915. The 2nd Battalion of the Black Watch was posted in Bareilly, India and was part of the Bareilly Brigade in the Meerut Division. They landed at Marseilles on 12 October 1914 and fought alongside the Indian regiments with some regularity.

(Above) Two sepoys shelter in a barn; one smokes a hookah. The sepoys, with their indigenous habits – such as smoking a hookah or washing with a *lota* (brass water mug) after a meal (below) were a source of much curiosity. These photographs were taken around the time of the Battle of Neuve-Chapelle (March 1915).

A wounded soldier is being stretchered by four orderlies. At the Battle of Neuve-Chapelle in March 1915, the Indian army sustained terrible casualties. The wounded were transported first to Boulogne by hospital ship and then to hospitals in the south of England.

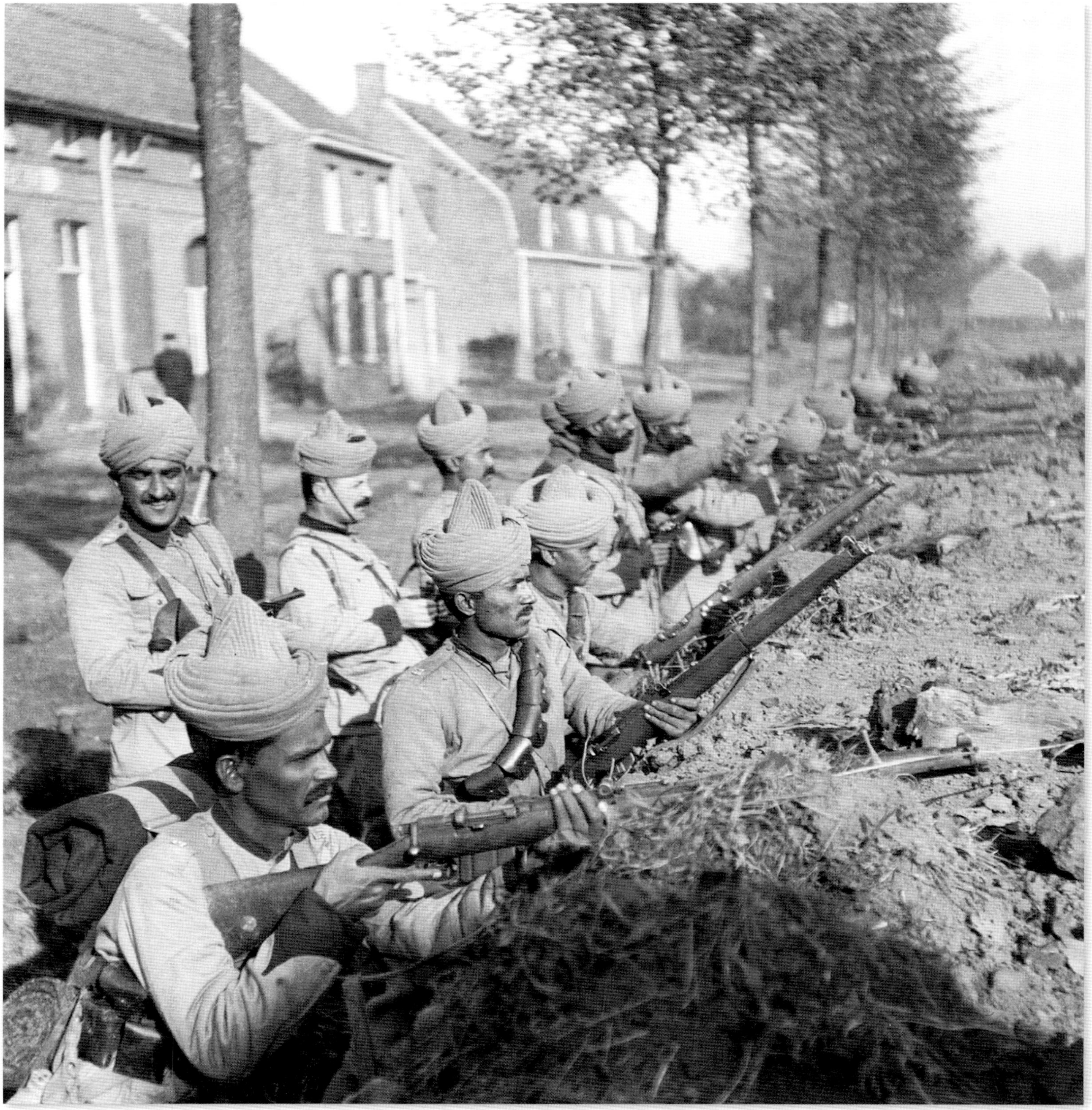

Viceroys Commissioned Officers (VCOs) and other ranks of the 57th Wilde's Rifles take aim in the trenches on the outskirts of Wytschaete, Belgium. The row of houses just behind them, showing the sepoys' close proximity to the town, exists even today on the outskirts of Ypres.

Sikh sepoys in the Army Cycle Corps at the crossroads between Fricourt and Mametz, France. Soldiers in the Cycle Corps had specially adapted bicycles that enabled them to carry their equipment. In the muddy trench warfare of the Western Front, however, bicycles proved less than practical.

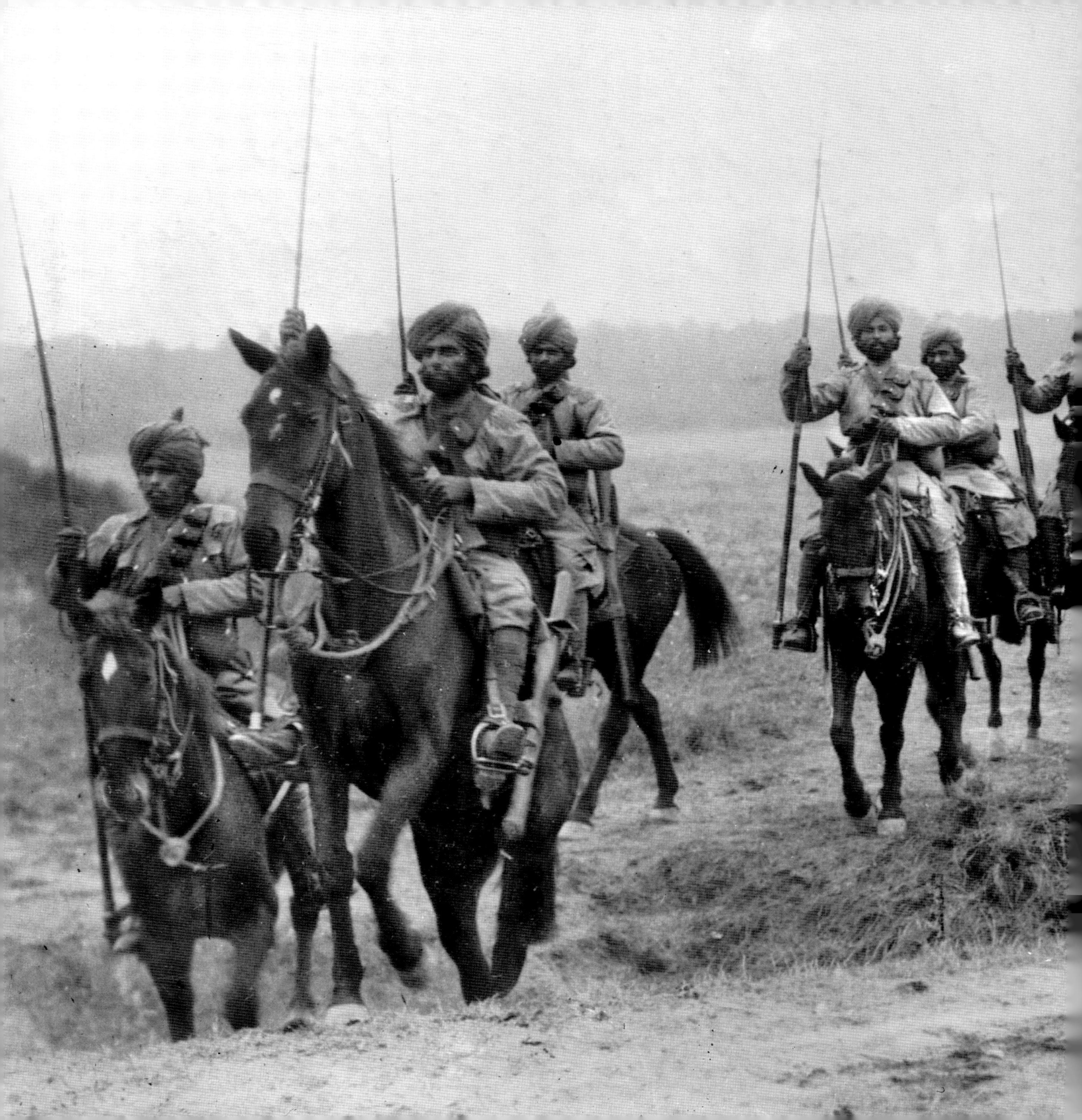

A detachment of Indian cavalry riding through the fields. Captain Roly Grimshaw, an officer with the 34th Poona Horse, wrote in his diary on 19 December 1914: 'Firstly for two months we had never fought on our horses or with them.' The Indian cavalry stayed in France till early 1918 but did not see any mounted action. Their moment came when they were transferred to Egypt and took part in the Battle of Haifa in September 1918.

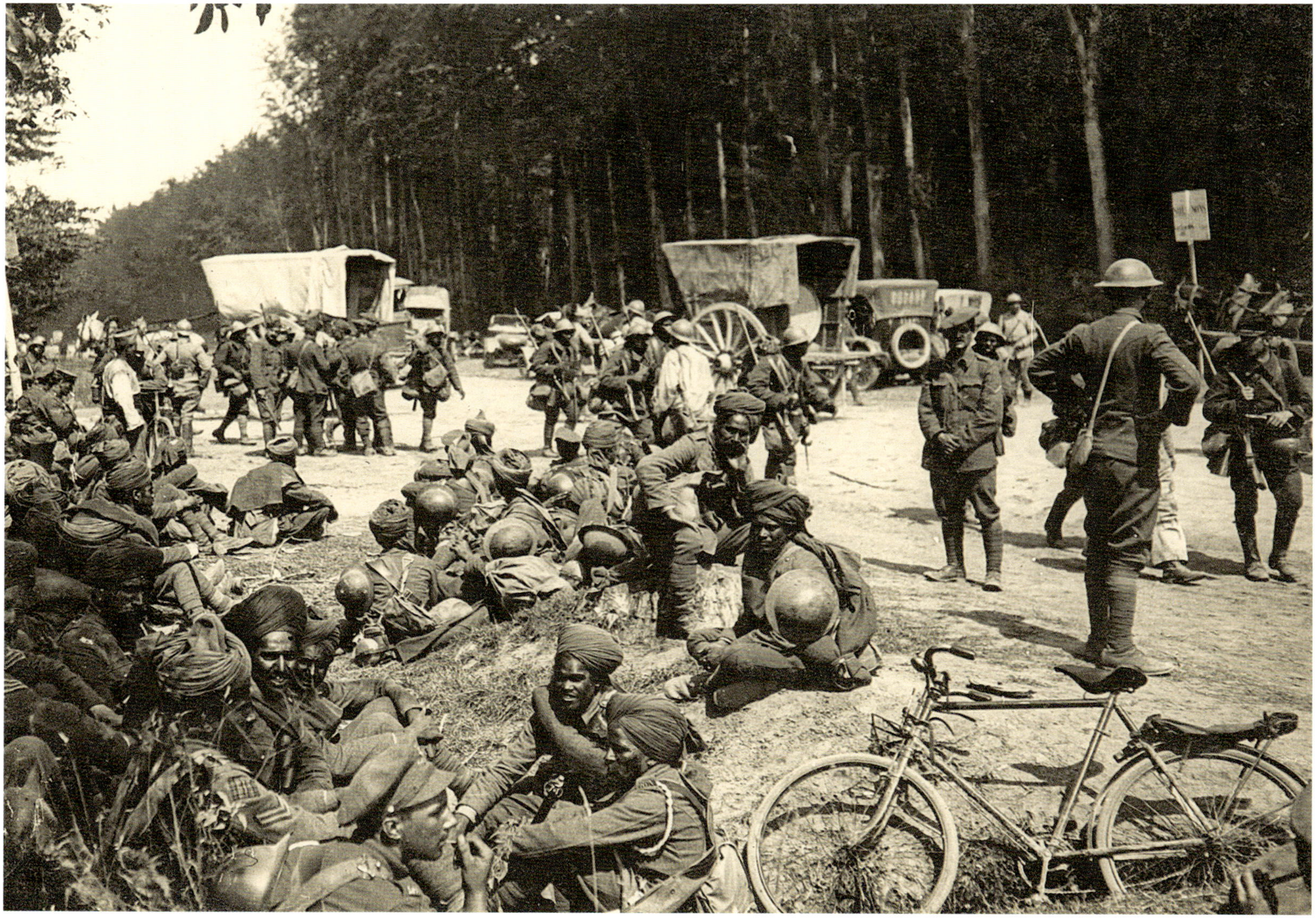

If the war was a clash of empires, it was also a space of encounter and contact. Knots of Allied soldiers – mainly French, Scottish and Indian – wait together and interact at a roadside crossing. On their way to relieving the Franco-American troops, the Indian troops had stopped on the road from Villers-Cotterêts to Soissons, 21 july 1918. More than one million non-white men passed through France alone during the war years.

(Above) Daily life at Gerbéviller, 1917. Members of the Indian cavalry share a moment of bonhomie as they relax in an old barn. In Anand's *Across the Black Waters*, the troops sing a Punjabi song as they sit together: 'Only four days to play, Oh mother, only four days to play!/Night has fallen, mother, my Beloved is far away'.

(Right) These striking photographs (p79, 81, 82, 83) were taken by Jean Segaud. Three sepoys sit in front of a train and pose while one draws on a hookah pipe. A Punjabi Muslim officer from 18th Lancers wrote on 20 February 1917: 'I have scrupulously performed all the necessary rites, prayer, charity and abstention from what is unlawful; but, through weakness, the flesh is now beginning to assert itself.'

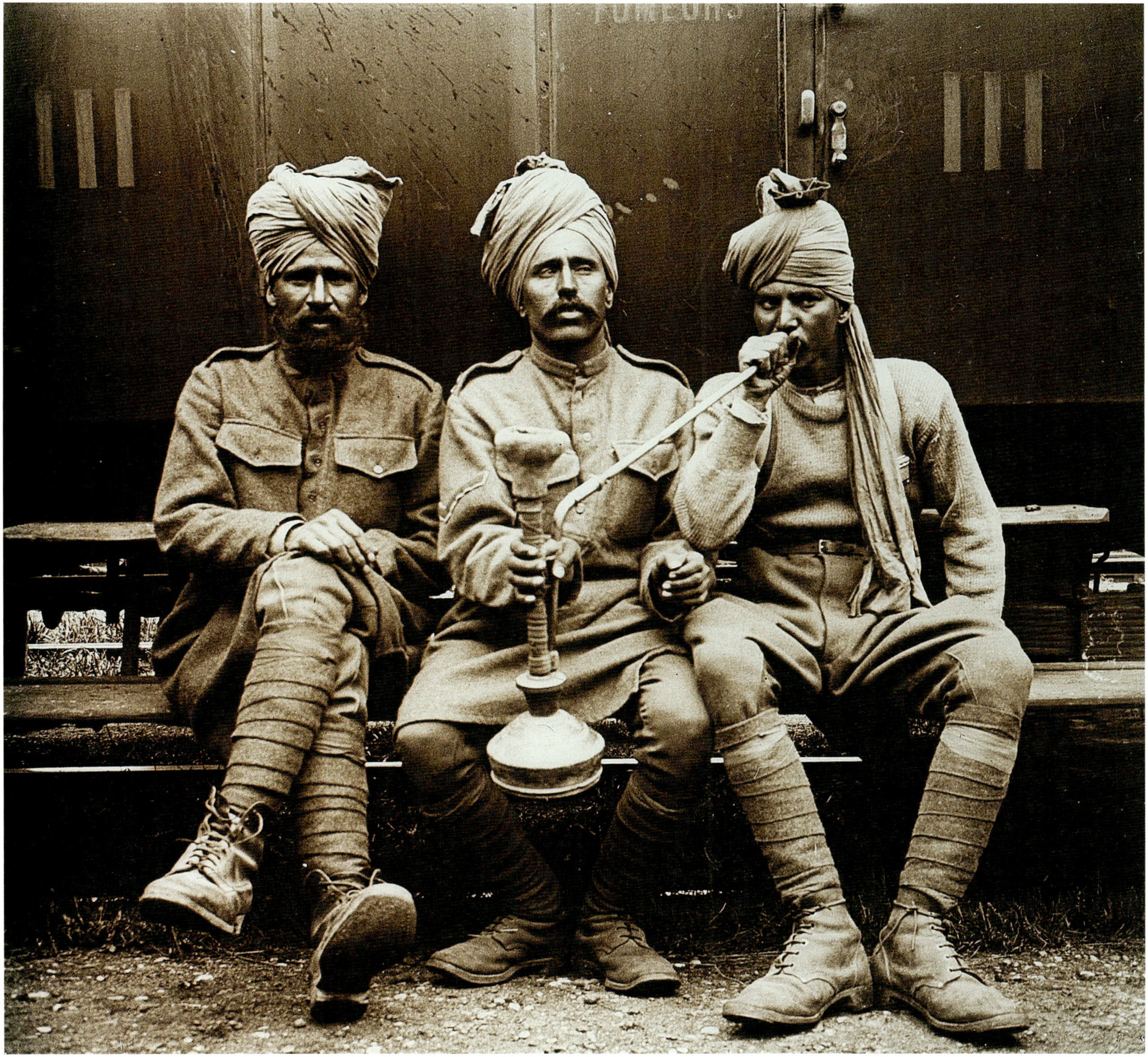

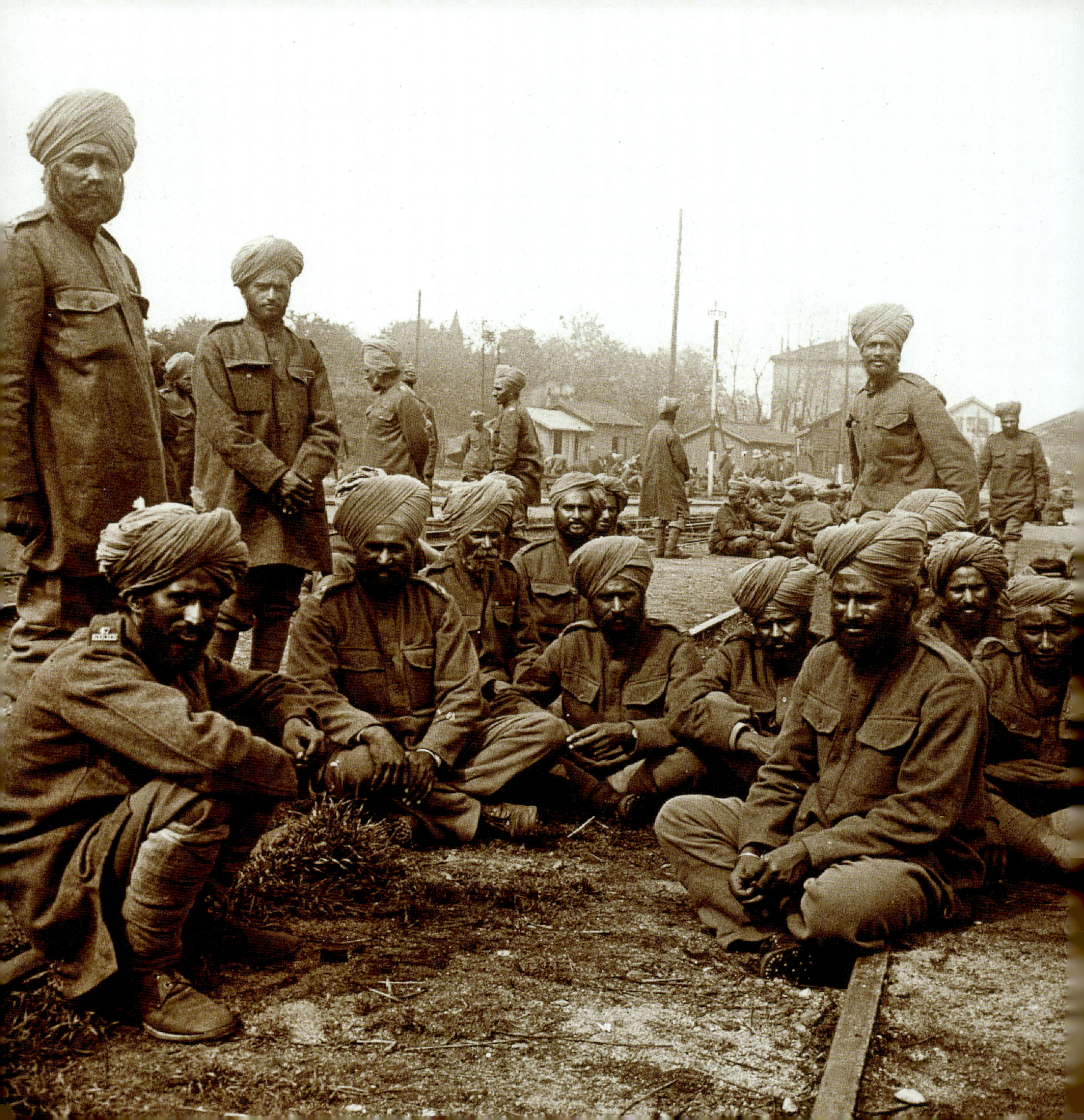

(Left) Knots of Sikh troops sit or stand on railway tracks while houses are visible in the background. It seems to be a snatched moment of rest at a major layover between their innumerable journeys.
(Above) Three uniformed Gurkhas pose in front of a train.

The Gurkhas from Nepal were considered to be 'warrior-gentlemen' of the Raj – the crème de la crème of the so-called 'martial races' along with the Jat Sikhs – and elicited a lot of interest from onlookers, photographers and writers.

(Following pages) The two pictures move between ethnology and voyeurism in their interest in the male body and its intimate processes of ablution and grooming.
(Left) Two sepoys are made to stand in symmetry and pose in the middle of their shower, caught between the gaze of the camera and the Europeans at the back. The stiffened posture of the man at the front shows his discomfort while the accoutrements of their shower – a bucket, *lota* and an open tap – are included to 'complete' the composition.
(Right) On the same spot, another man is made to stand and face the camera: he is more confident and relaxed, and is a Sikh with his long hair but without his turban.

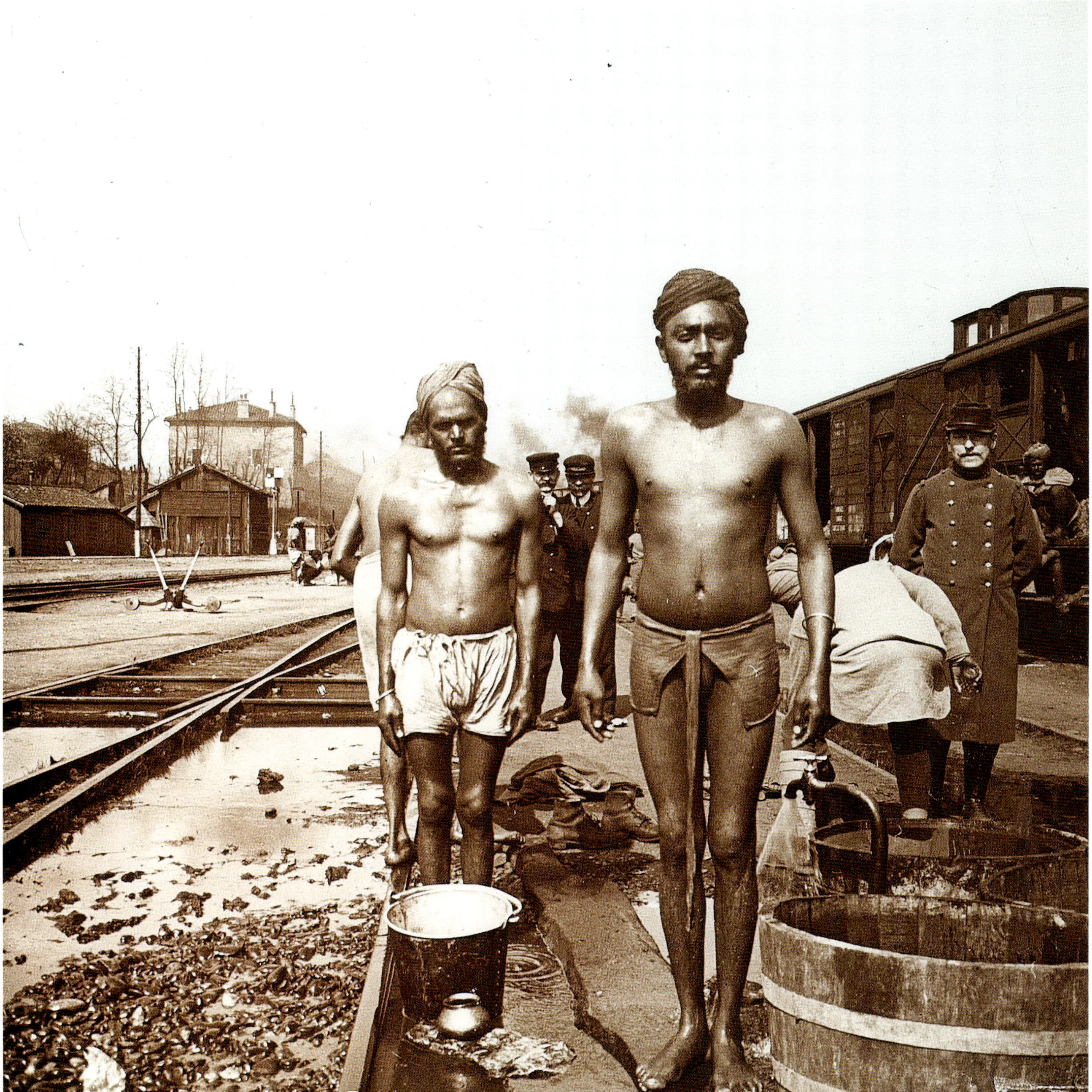

83

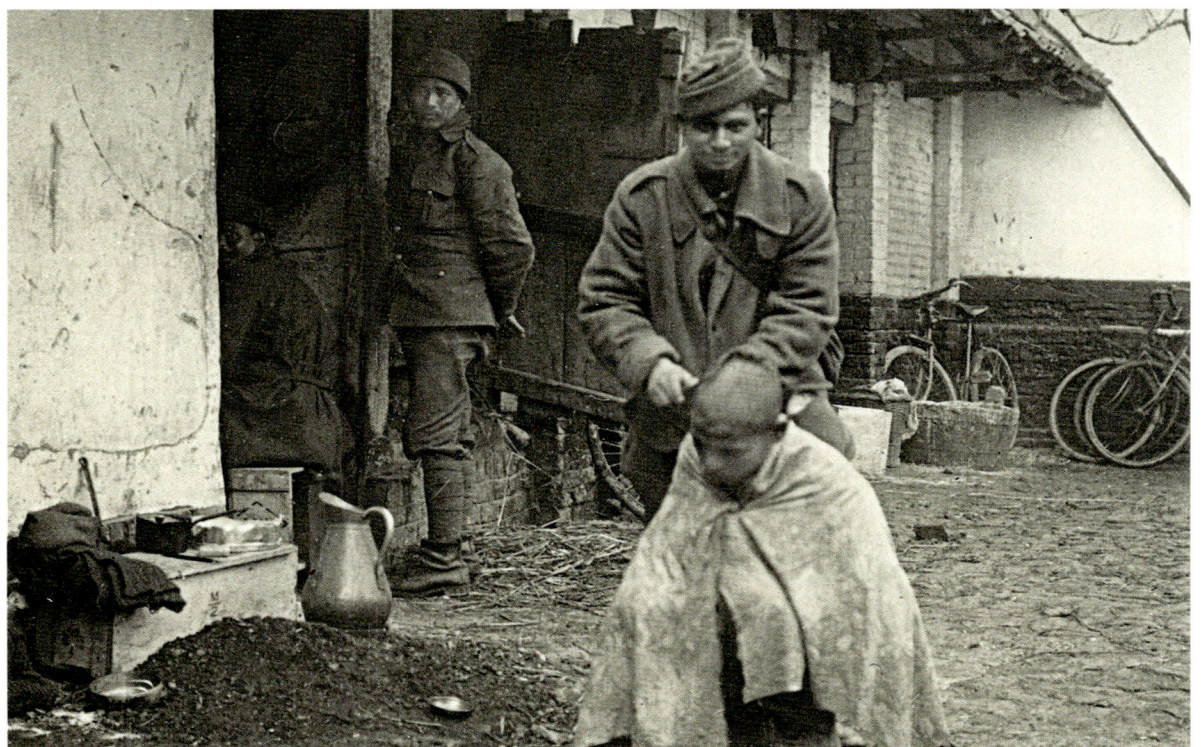

A large number of 'private' followers – *dhobis* (washermen), *langris* (cooks), barbers, tailors and blacksmiths – served the combatants. The photographs show at once an orientalist curiosity in the men and their everyday rituals in the Indian camp. (Above) A *dhobi* puts out clothes to dry. (Below) The barber is busy at work. (Right) A shared homosocial moment as a man with flamboyant moustache is being groomed while a *lota* or brass water-vessel lies by his side. The sitting postures of the two men suggest a history of bodily gestures different from those of Europeans and fascinated artists such as Paul Sarrut; they also capture how these men created a little 'India' on French fields.

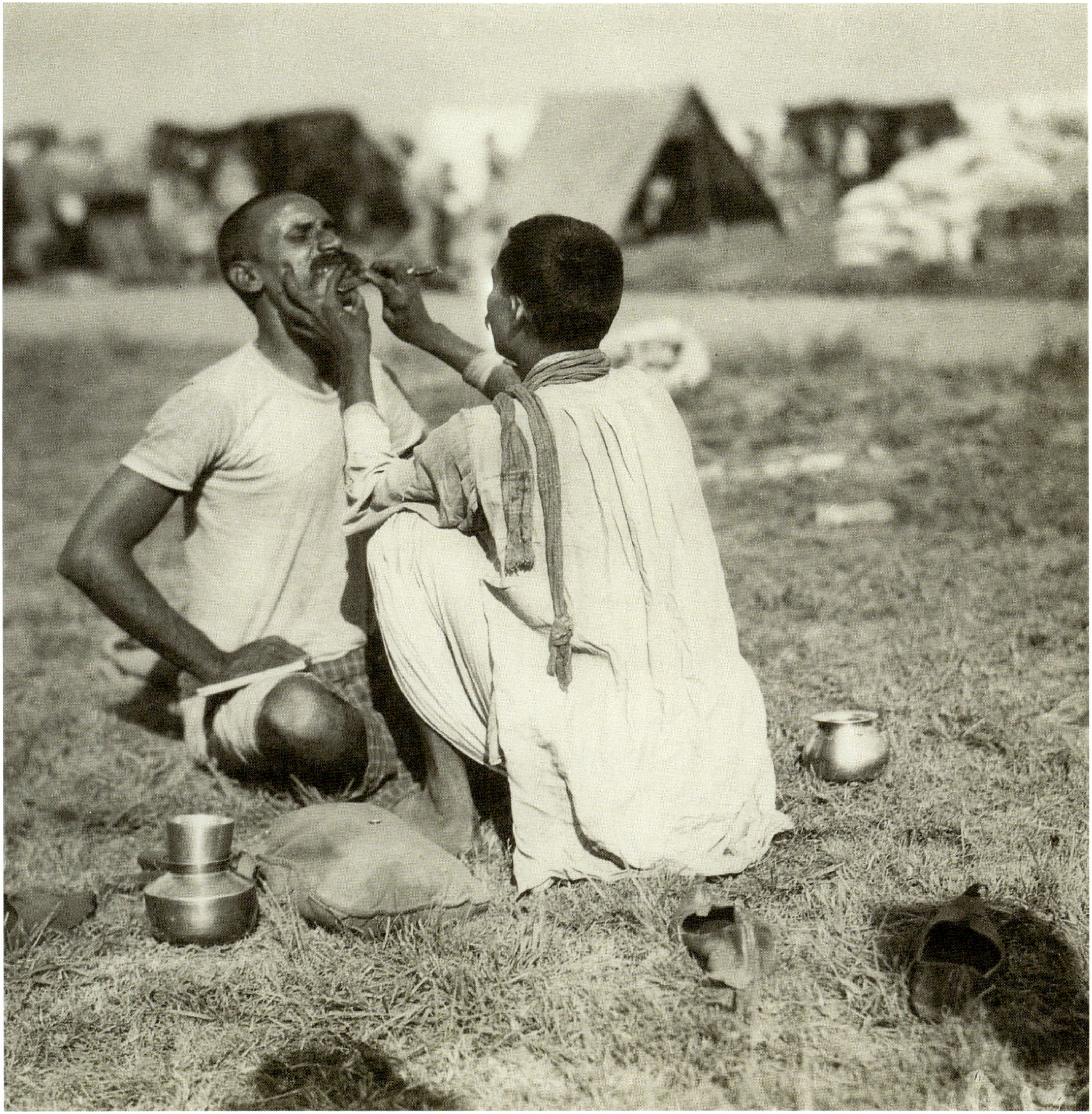

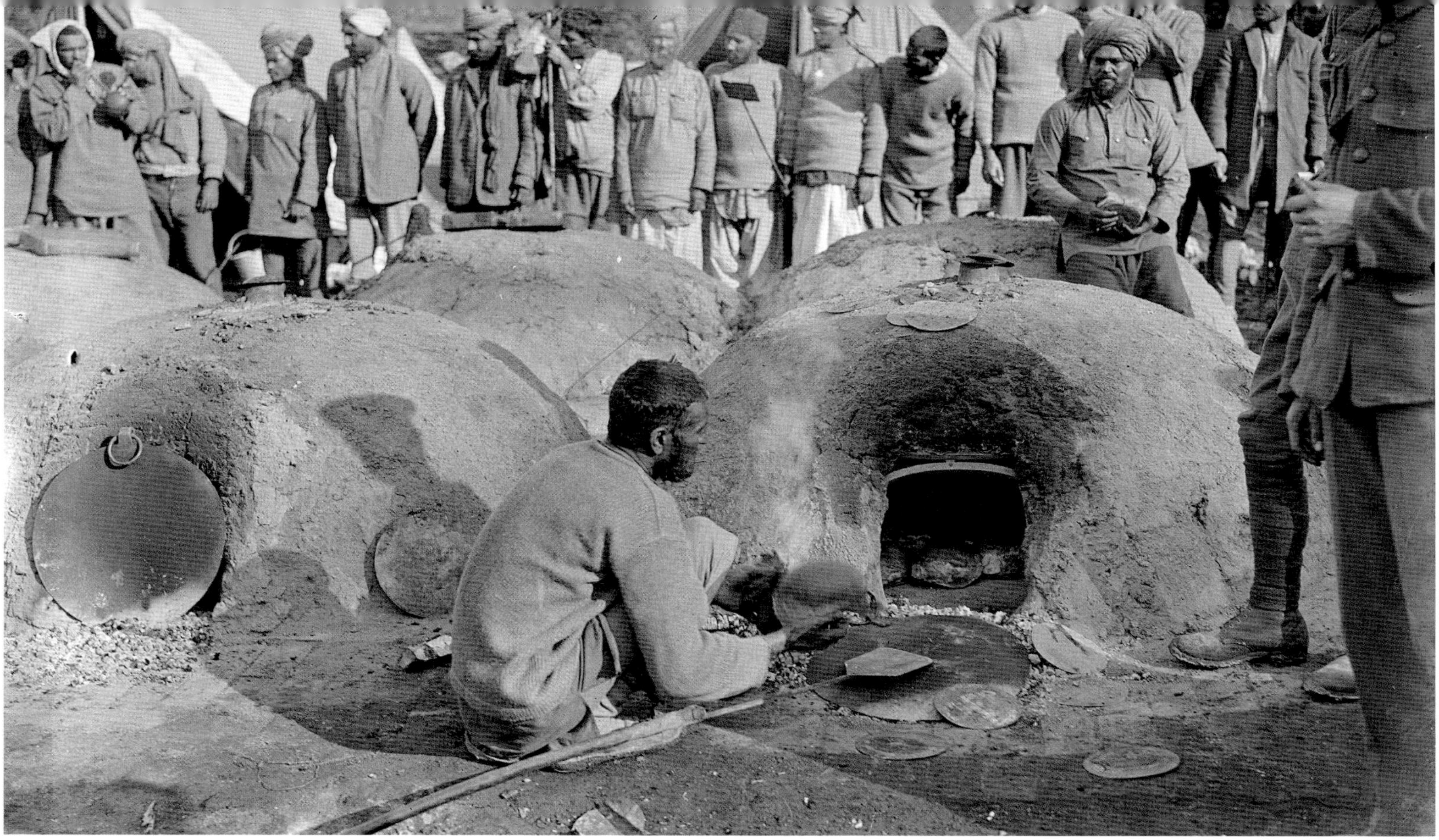

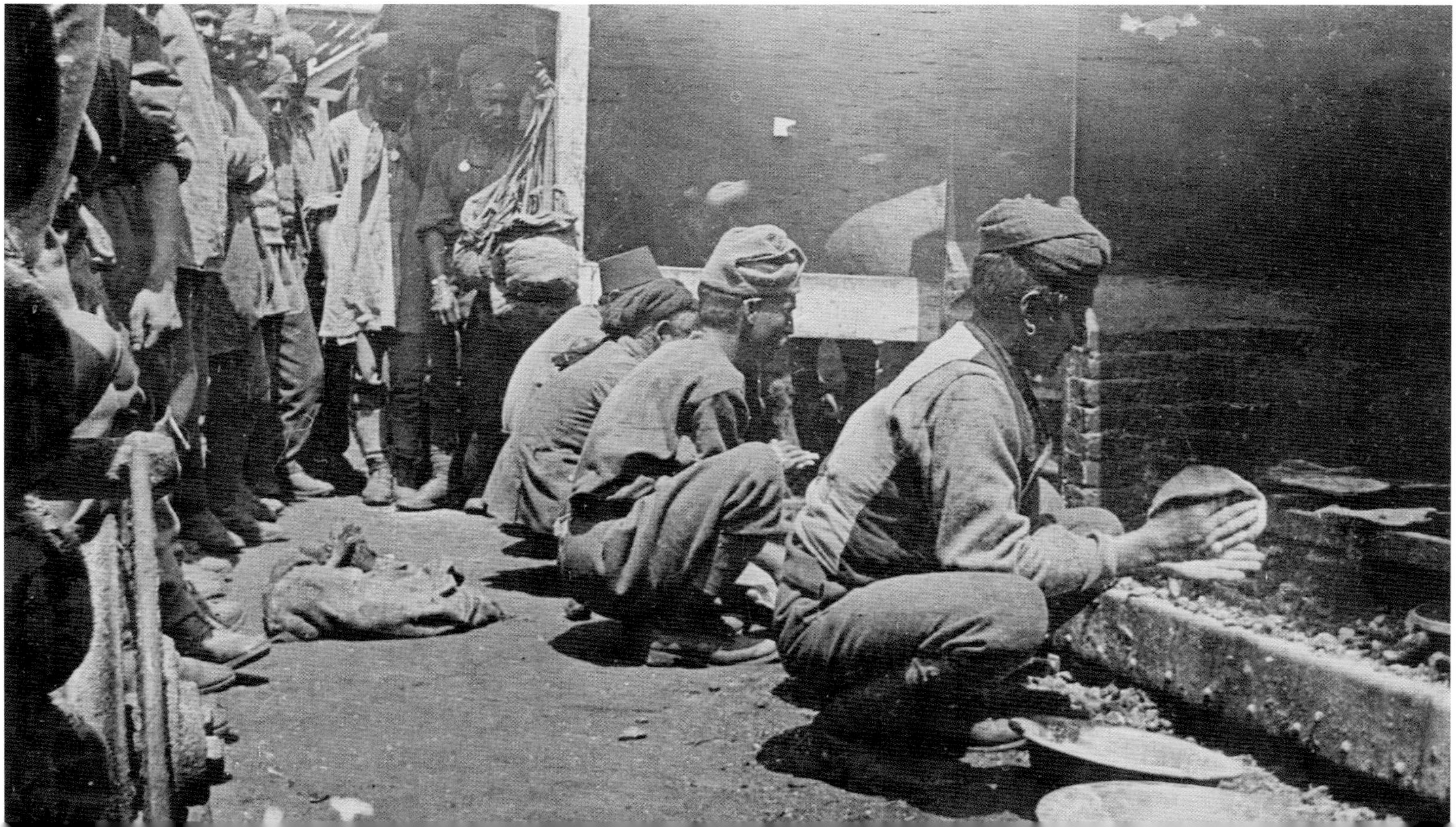

Elaborate arrangements were made for cooking at Orléans. (Left) Chapattis are being prepared while a cook sits on his haunches in front of an improvised oven in the Orléans camp, November 1914. On 6 June 1915, Father Van Walleghem, a Belgian priest, wrote in his diary: 'The Indians bake a kind of pancake and also eat a kind of seed with a very strong taste.' The Indian ration in 1914 comprised 1/4 pound meat, 1/8 pound potatoes, 1/3 ounce tea, 1/2 ounce salt, 1 1/2 pound *atta* (flour), 4 ounces *dhal* (lentil soup), 2 ounces ghee (clarified butter), 1/6 ounce chillies, 1/6 ounce turmeric, 1/3 ounce ginger, 1/6 ounce garlic and 1 ounce *gur* (molasses).

(Above) Homesick? Alone in the field, a man looks plaintive as he eats his chapattis by himself. 'We get warm *parathas* [chapattis fried in oil] and meat twice a day', wrote a sepoy from France to his father in December 1915: he may be exaggerating to keep his parents from worrying.

88

Controversy over meat erupted in october 1914 when the 47th Sikhs were given lamb mince but in a tin with a picture of a cow! For Muslim troops, halal practices for meat were introduced, causing considerable curiosity from onlookers. (Left) Goats are being slaughtered according to the halal method. (Above) A man cooks on a makeshift oven.

Indian troops marching as part of the annual Bastille Day Parade in the Champs-Elysées, in Paris. These photographs were taken on 14th July 1916 – the Battle of the Somme had already begun on the Western Front.
(Right) A French lady gives flowers to a Viceroy's Commissioned Officer.

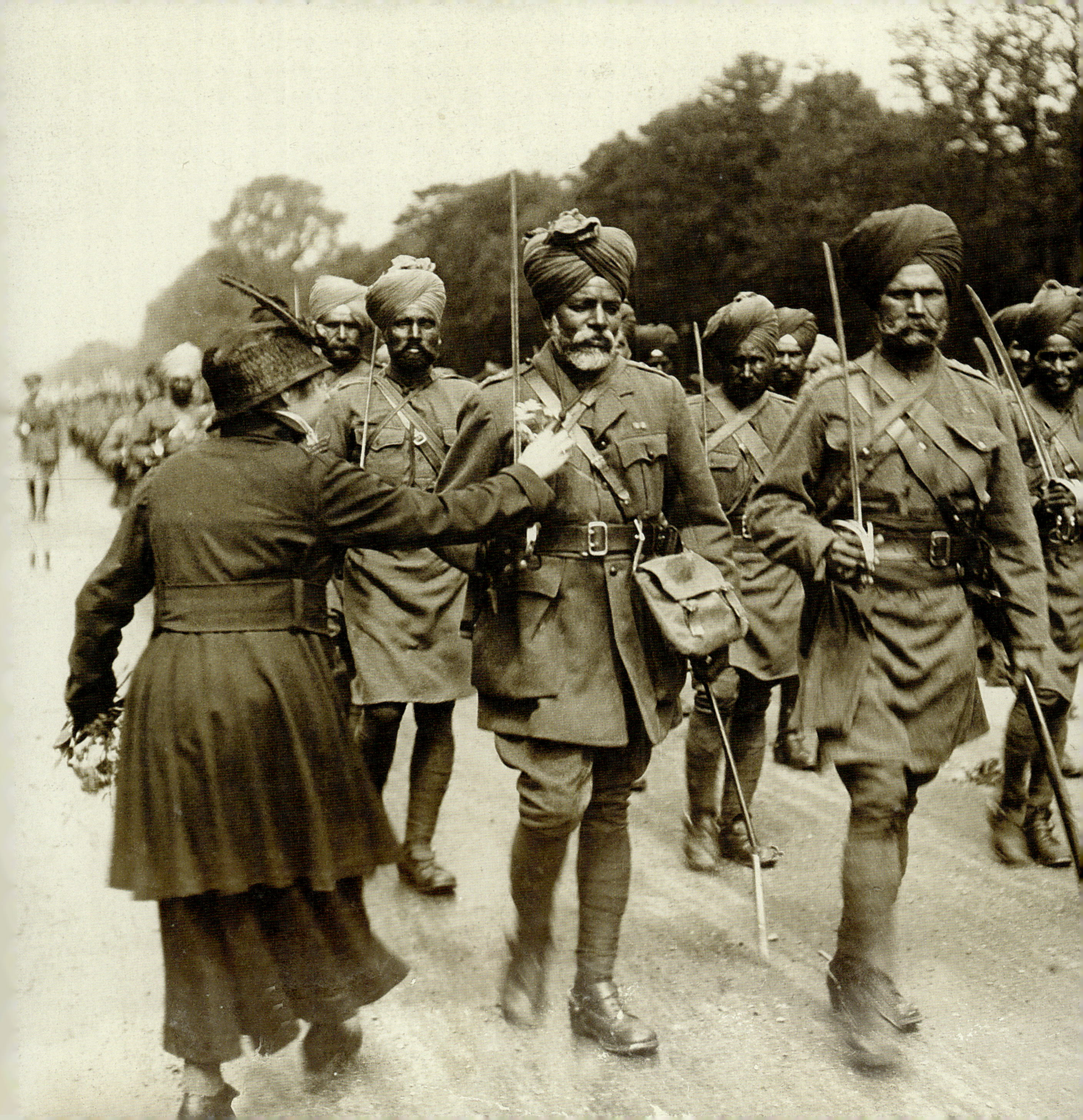

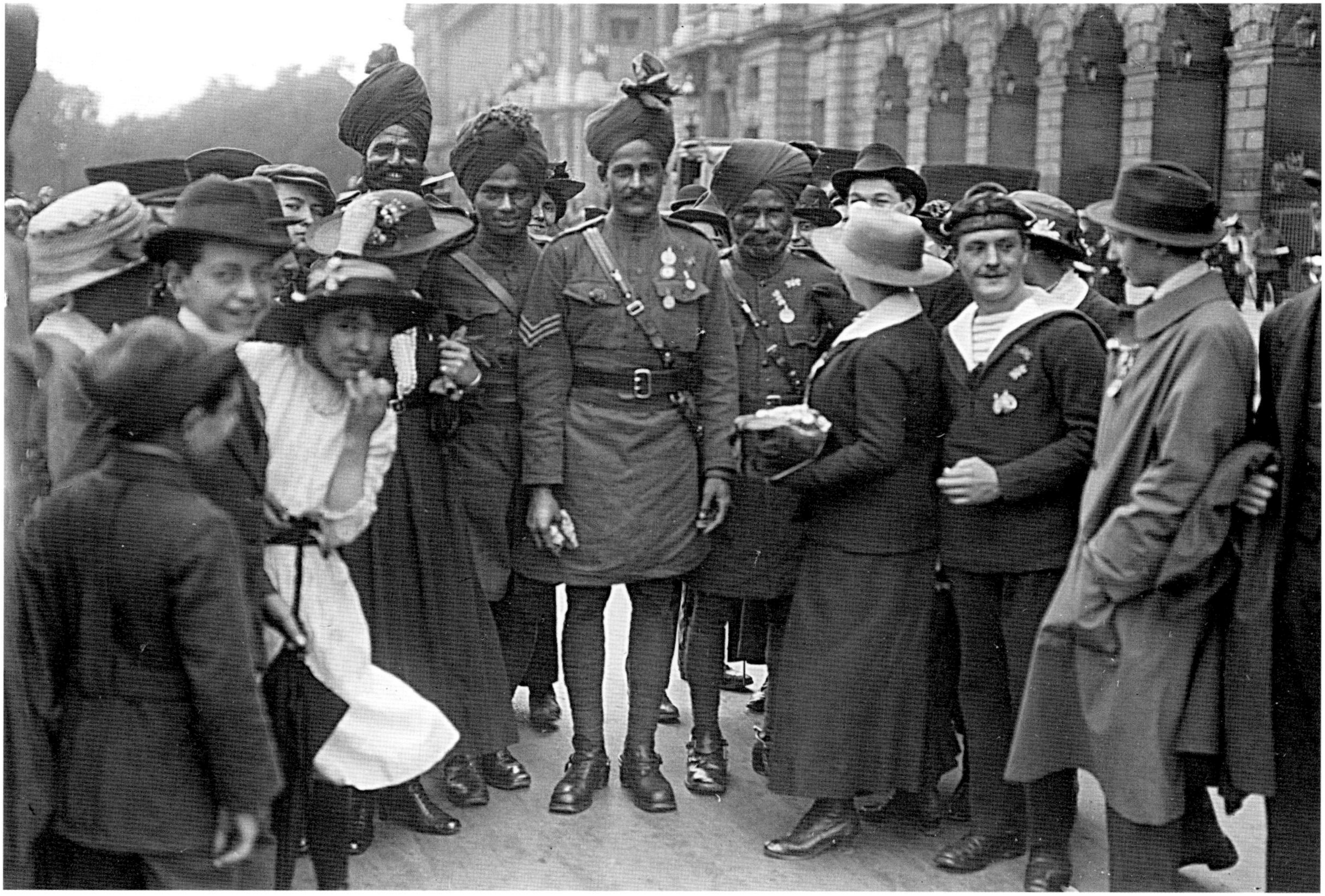

(Left) Excited Parisians surround and cheer the Indian sepoys after the Bastille Day Parade: they are keen to be part of the historical – and photographic – moment. (Right) A statuesque Sikh sepoy leads the way, acknowledging the adulation with a triumphant wave. Many sepoys harboured a soft spot for Paris, comparing the city to a 'fairyland' and calling its people the most beautiful in the world.

Soldiers in their letters repeatedly mention their encounters with the local children. (Left) The above postcard shows sepoys being followed by local children. (Right) A Sepoy places a turban on the girl's head. The postcard was possibly used to propagate 'Indo-European' bonds in times of war.
(Right) A Pathan soldier takes some food from a basket offered by a local Frenchwoman in 1915.

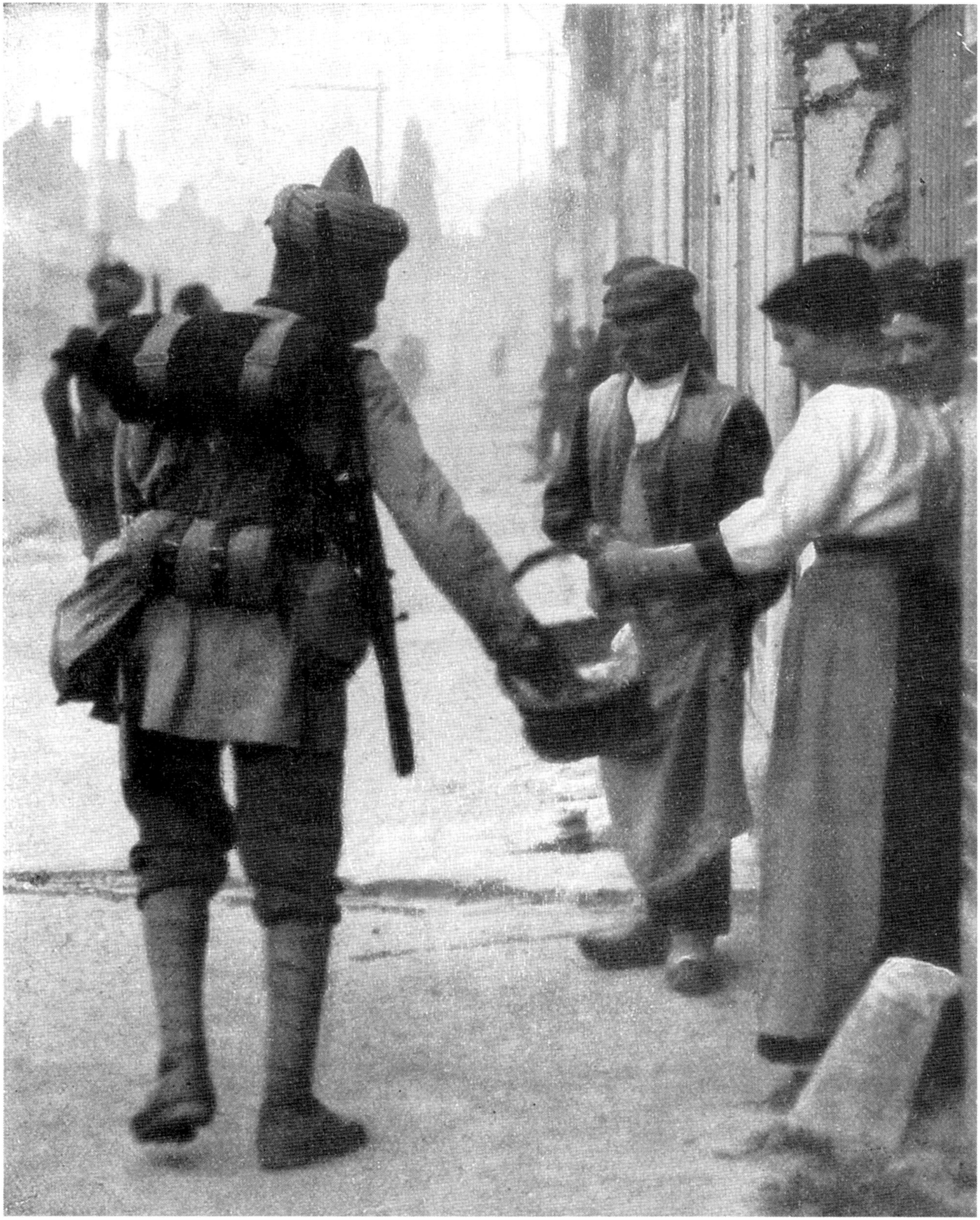

Two sepoys billeted at a farm in northern France pose with members of the family. One of the soldiers seems to have written his name, age (25) and possibly village (Ferozepore) at the back of the card, showing a certain degree of familiarity with the English script. On 9 January 1916, a sepoy by the name of Sher Bahadur Khan wrote to his family: 'There are miles of difference between the women of India and the women of this country. During the whole three months I never saw this old lady sitting idle, although she belonged to a high family. Indeed, during the whole three months, she ministered to me to such an extent that I cannot adequately describe her [kindness].'

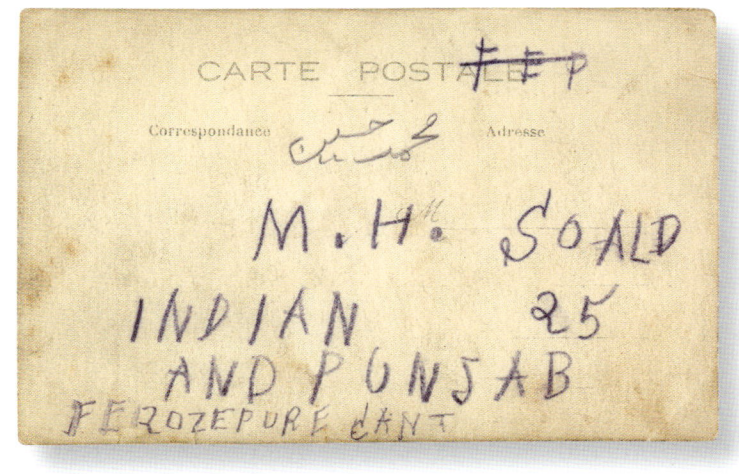

A possibly staged but poignant image of a sepoy from the 15th Ludhiana Sikhs with a small boy while the others look on. Anand, in *Across the Black Waters*, writes: 'The children laughed at the incomprehensible speech of the sepoys and the sepoys laughed back and cheered them with a crude bluff of tenderness for the little ones.'

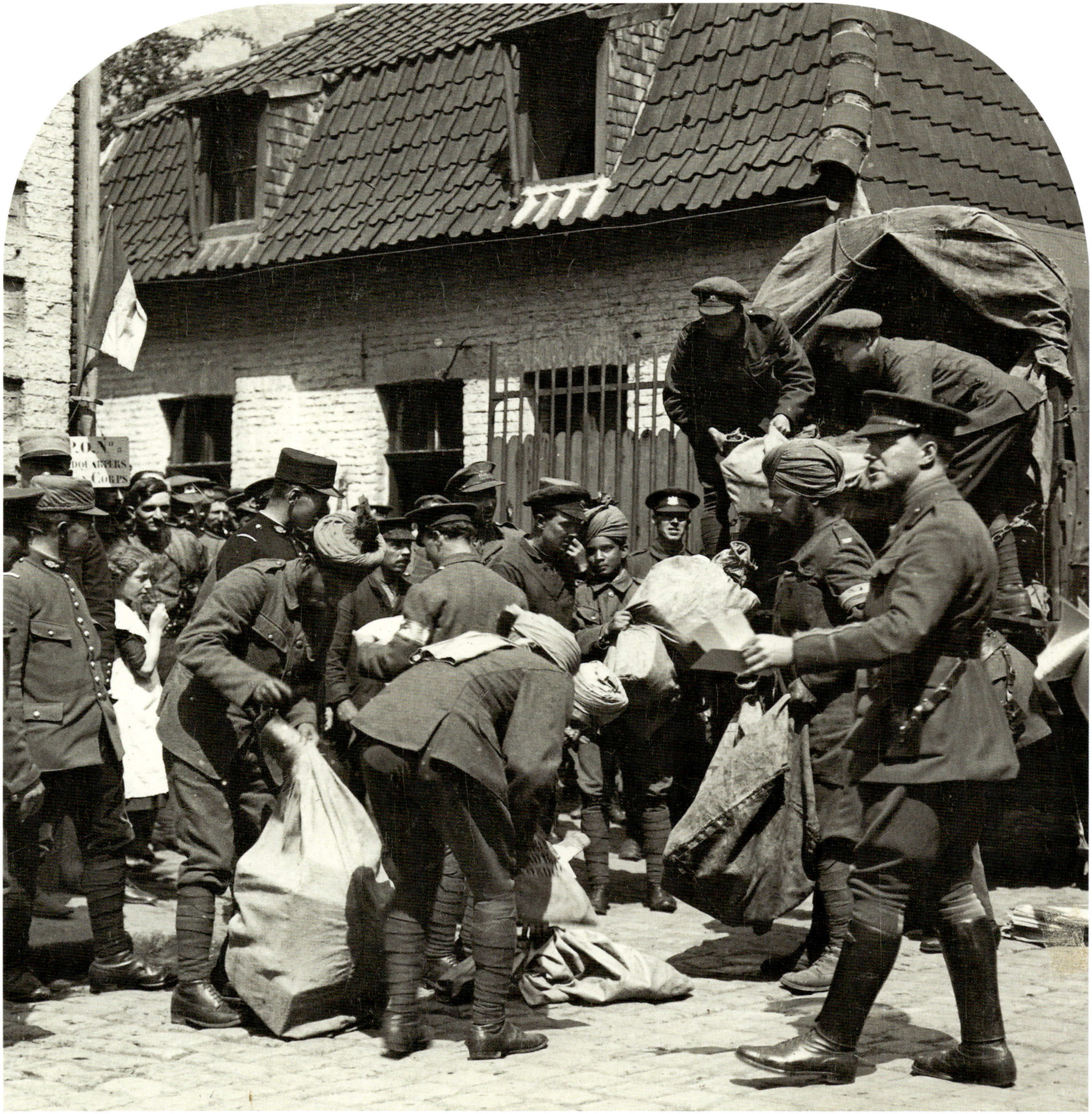
CORPS

A field post office. The literacy rate in the Punjab was around 5% but, by 1915, the Indians were writing (or dictating) 10,000–20,000 letters per week. 'Oh happy paper, how I envy your lot. We shall be here but you will go and see [India]', exclaims a sepoy in Pashtu in a letter otherwise written in Urdu. The officer in the foreground was killed the next day. A very young Indian boy with a bag of letters in his hand as well as a young European girl can be seen amidst the crowd at the back.

(Right, above) A British officer overseeing the work of two Indian clerks who are going through the mail. The translator or censor would dutifully extract passages from the sepoys' letters to be sent to the Chief Censor. (Right, below) Members of the Burmese Labour Corps near Contalmaison reading newspapers delivered from India. Such photographs show that not all sepoys and labourers were non-literate: some learnt to read and write in the regimental schools and some even picked up a little French.

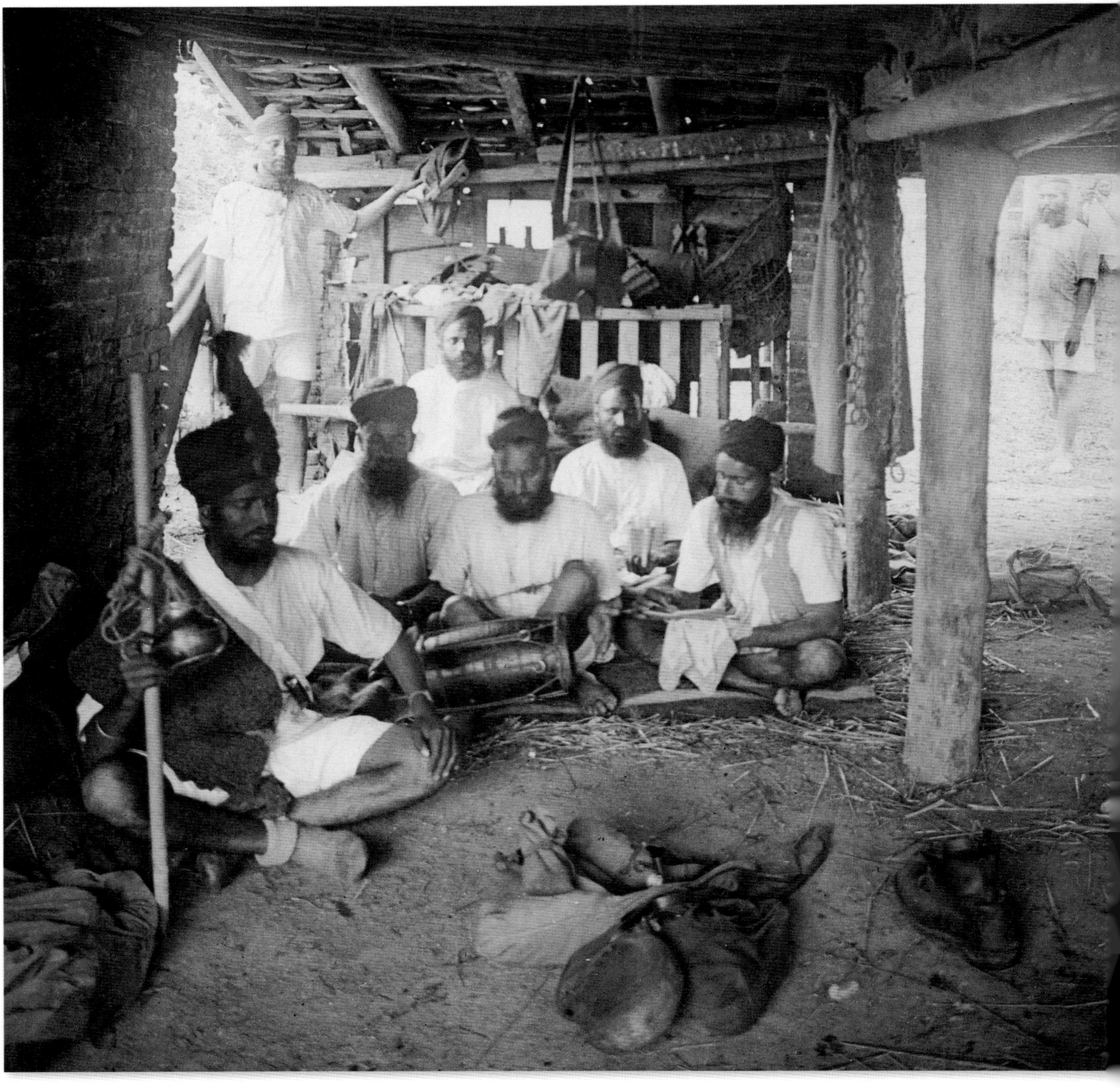

(Left) A group of Sikh soldiers sit at their daily prayer which involved reading, recitation or singing of hymns. There was a vibrant oral culture in the Punjab – in terms of chants, hymns, prayers, songs – which the sepoys brought to France. One plays the *dholak* while another reads from a religious text.

(Above) Indian Muslim troops kneel and pray outside the Shah Jahan Mosque in Woking, Surrey, during the festival of Bakr Id (Eid al-Adha in Arabic) in 1916 as local people look on. It marks the willingness of Ibrahim to sacrifice his first-born son Ismail to the will of God, before God intervened and provided a lamb (*bakr*) to sacrifice instead.

102

During the four years of war, India sent abroad around 172,815 animals, including horses, mules and ponies, camels, draught bullocks and dairy cattle. These included ponies and mules, sometimes obtained from abroad but trained in India before being shipped abroad. (Left) The mules are having a 'dustbath'. (Above) Sikh sepoys wait around with mules in their camp; Indian cavalry horse hospitals were also set up in France.

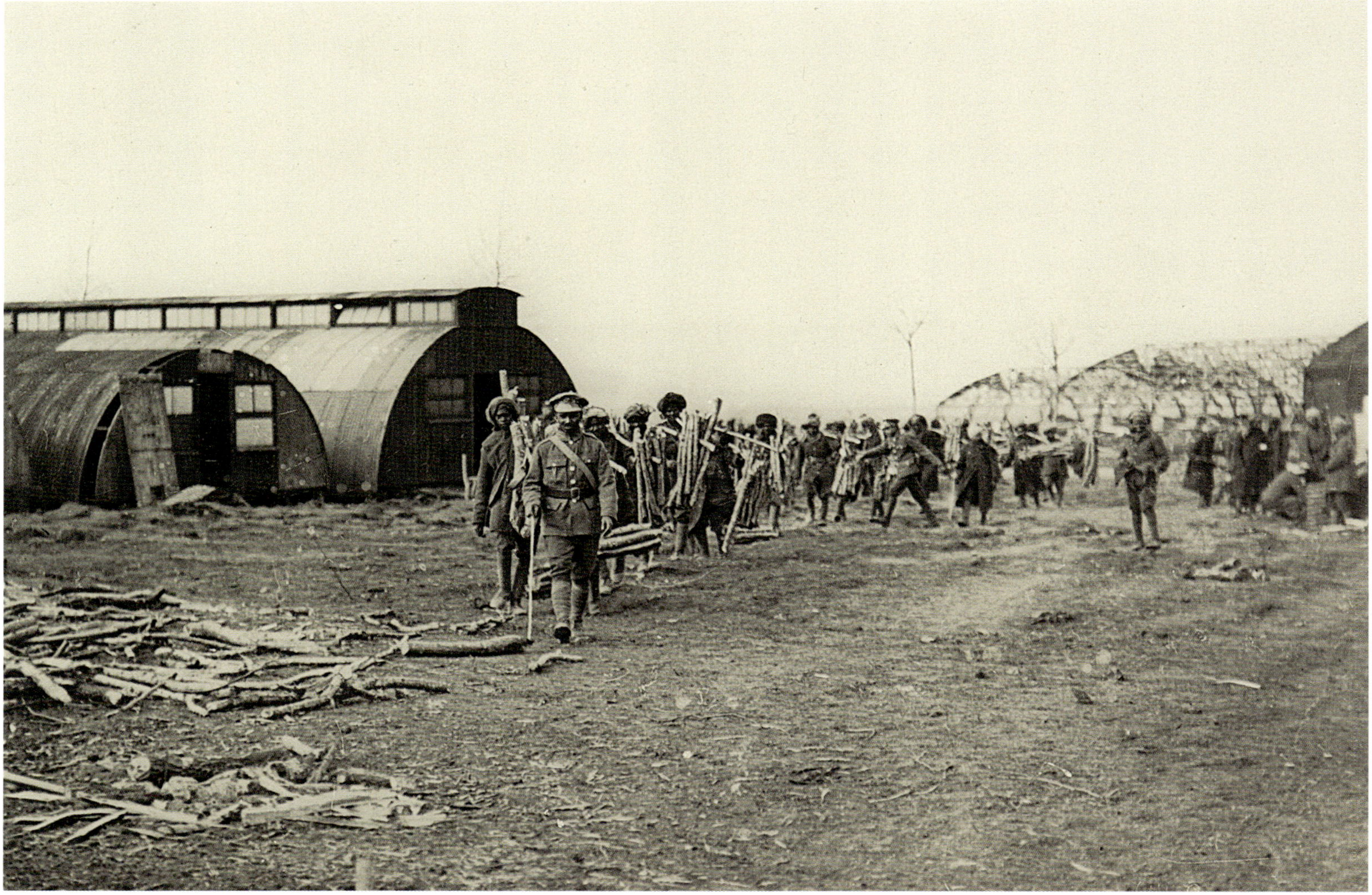

Indian Labour Corps working on a construction site for a British aerodrome in February 1918 at Azelot, north-eastern France. Royal Flying Corps squadrons 55, 99 and 104 were based at the aerodrome. Maurice Baring, private secretary to the commander of the Royal Flying Corps in France, remembered that 'it was bitterly cold' and 'an aerodrome was being made out of what looked like a Scotch moor, with the help of some Indian troops'. There will be up to 150 british bombers parked on this airfield.

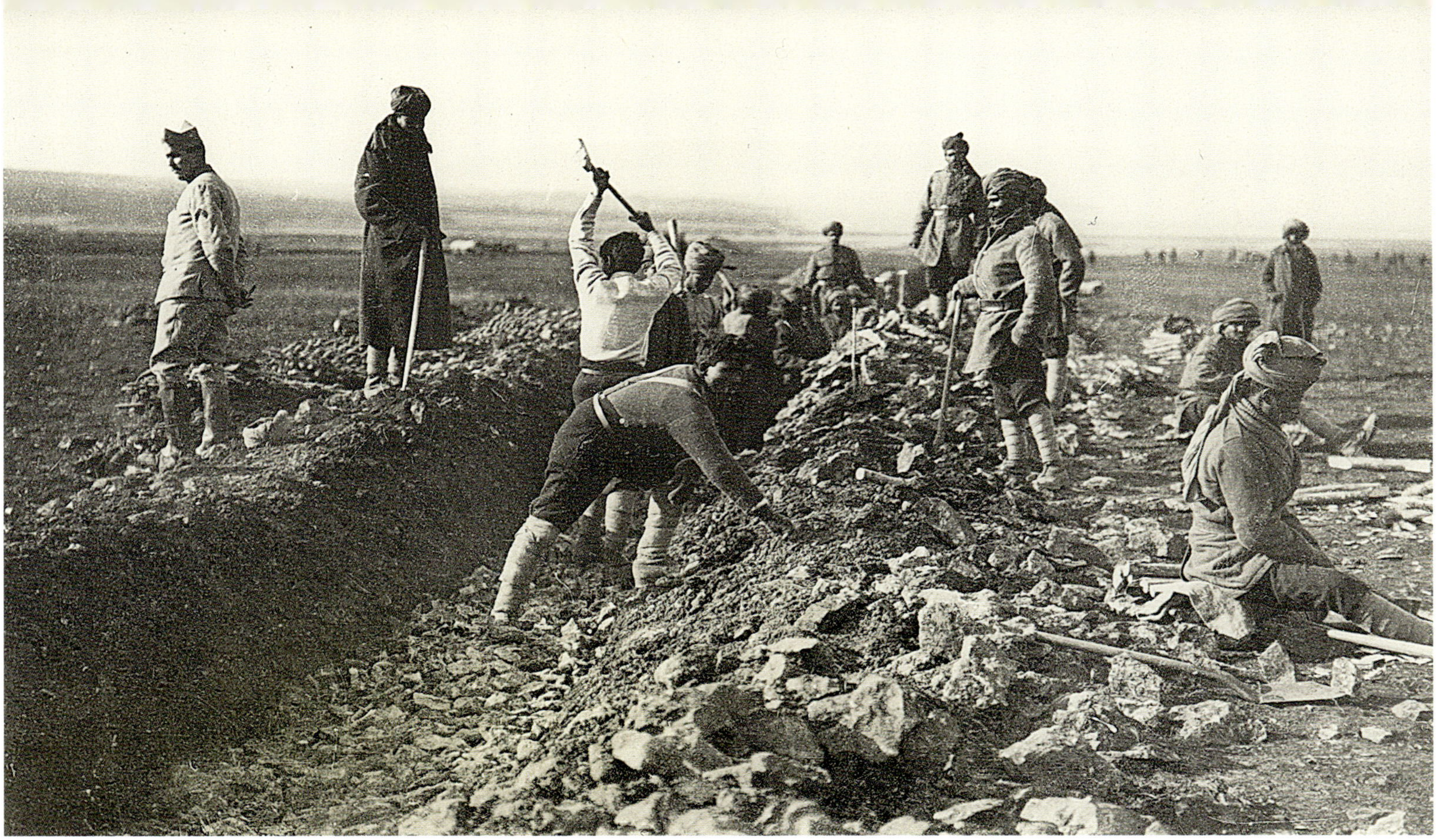

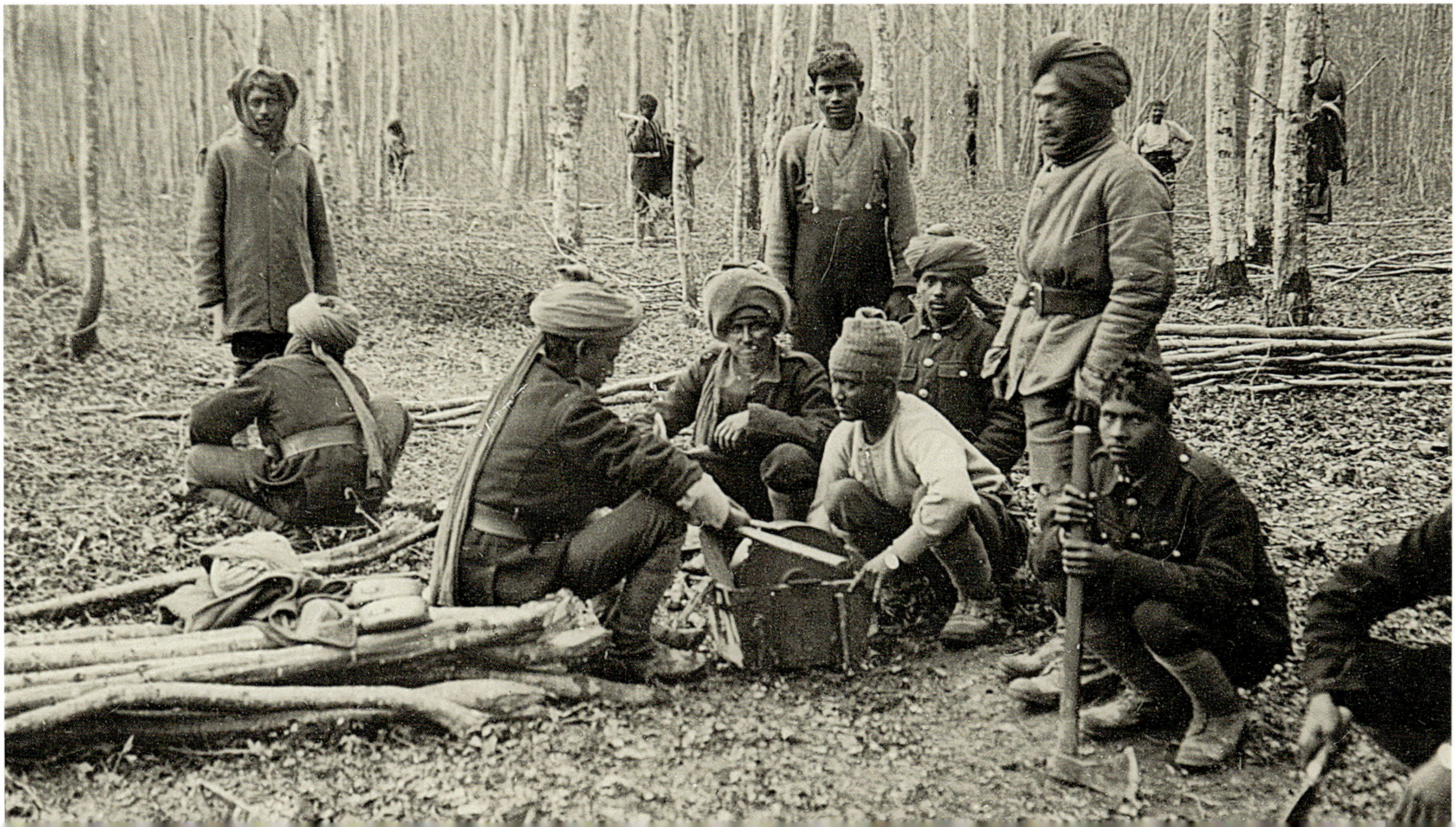

Construction-fodder: Indian Labour Corps hard at work, digging a drainage trench, felling trees and chopping wood, at Azelot amidst extreme cold in February 1918. The Commonwealth War Graves Commission lists the names of four members of the Indian Labour Corps – Bhima Paharia, Jadu Hembrom, Jummi and Sibu – all of whom died between February and April 1918 and were buried at the Azelot communal cemetery.
A labourer stands amidst the desolate landscape – perhaps taking a momentary break from work. He is wearing boots but no gloves.

(Above) The famous Sir Pertab Singh, the Regent of Jodhpur, with two Indian aristocratic officers. A favourite of Queen Victoria, the 70-year-old Sir Pertab was said to have threatened to sit at the doorstep of the Viceroy in protest if not allowed to serve in the war. He served in Europe 1914–1915 and then in Haifa and Aleppo.

(Right) Their uniforms blending with the camouflage, two Indian officers, including the Maharajah of Patiala Bhupinder Singh, and a British officer inspect an artillery weapon. A keen cricketer, the maharajah served in France, Belgium, Italy and Palestine as an honorary lieutenant colonel, and was promoted to the rank of honorary major-general in 1918.

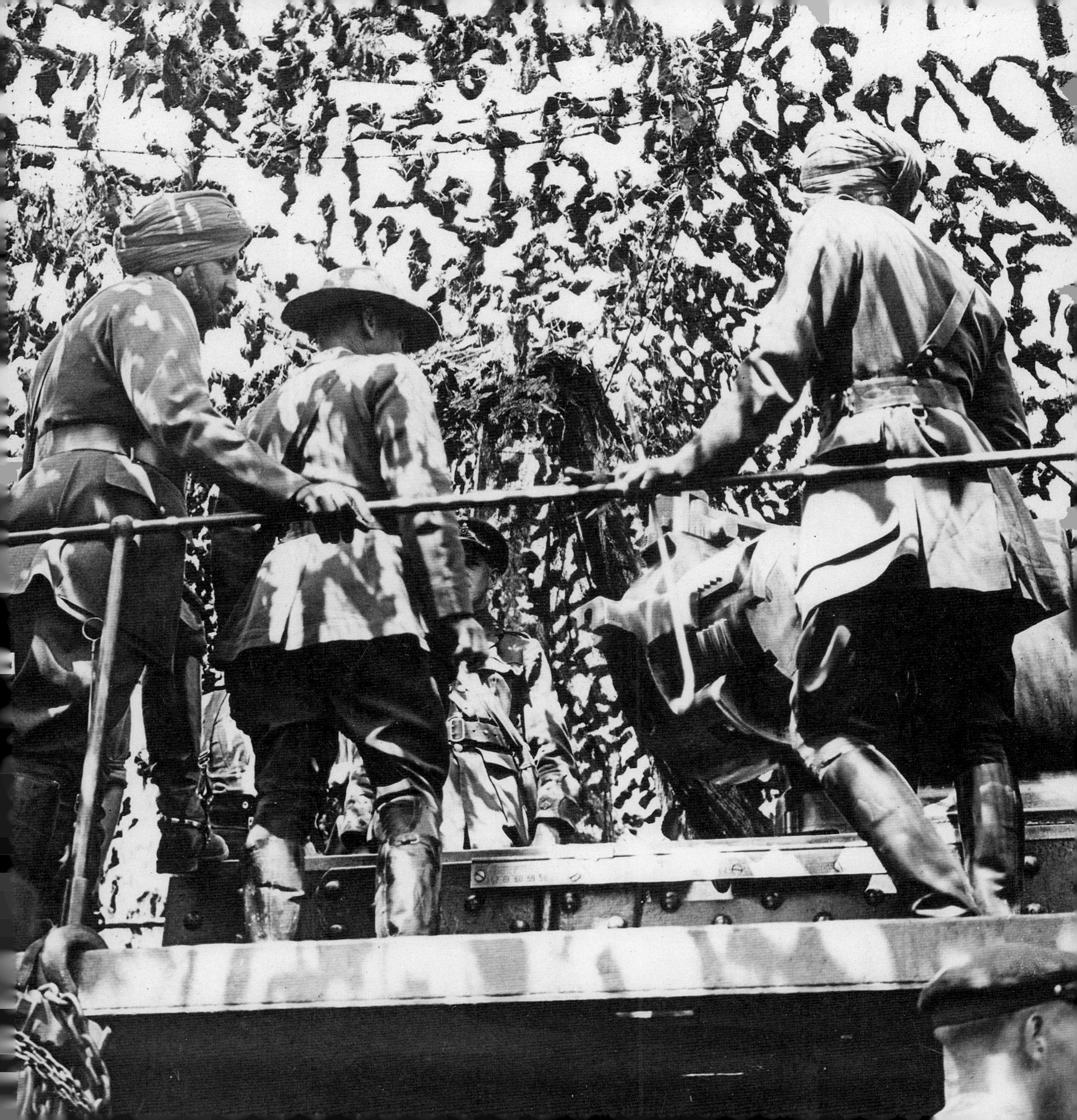

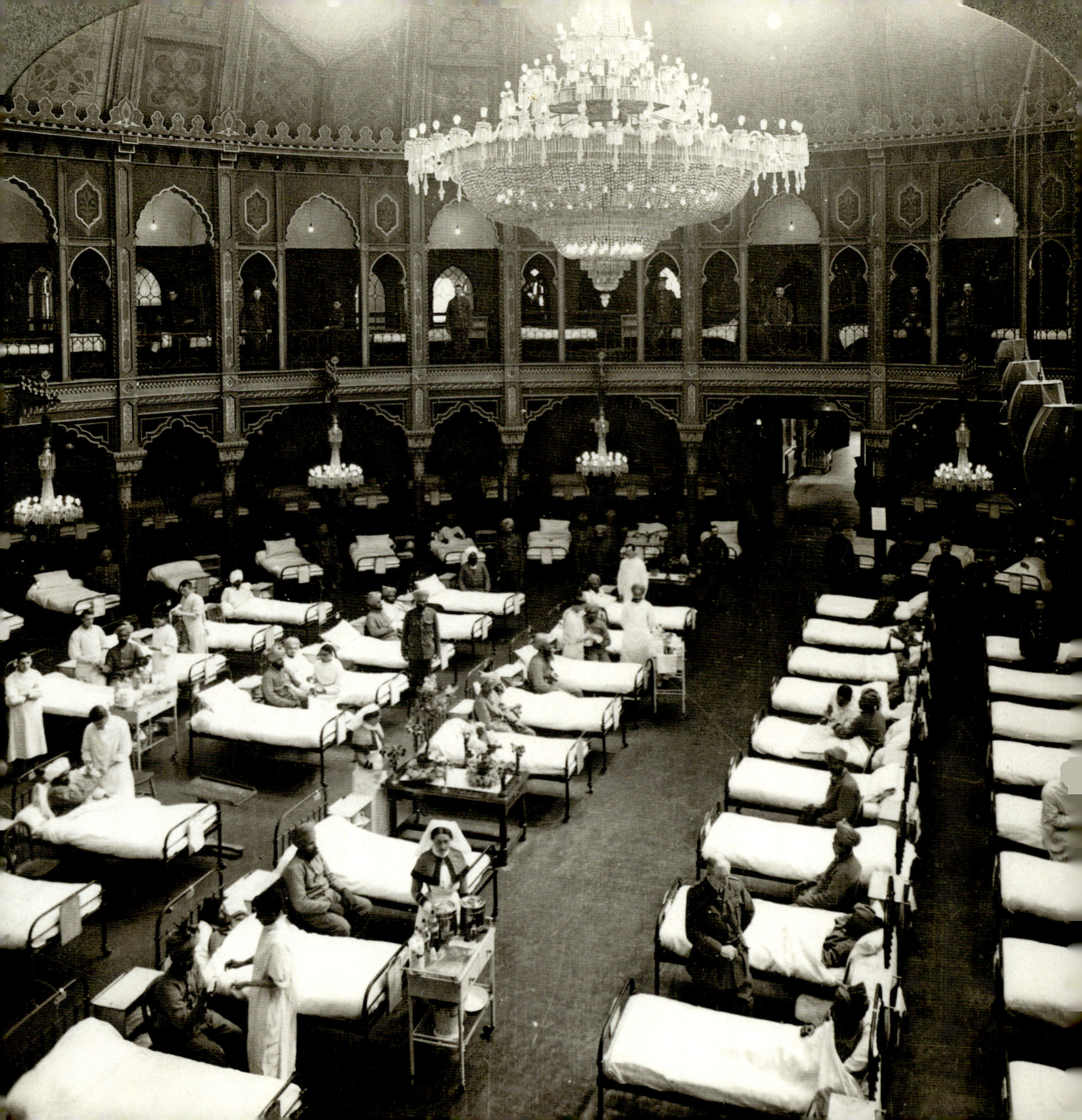

Hospitals

'I have been twice wounded, once in the left hand, of which two fingers are powerless. The other injury is from gas – that is dhua [smoke]. It gives me great pain and will go on doing so ... I have got the Victoria Cross.' So wrote Subedar Mir Dast, VC, on 12 July 1915 from his hospital bed at the Brighton Pavilion Hospital in England.[1] Wounded and gassed at the second battle of Ypres in April 1915, Mir Dast was the fourth Indian (and first Indian officer) to win the Victoria Cross. He continued, 'The Victoria Cross is a very fine thing, but this gas gives me no rest.'[2]

The Indian Corps on the Western Front suffered heavy casualties even before the regiment was properly entrenched. Shrapnel wreaked havoc in the opening months of combat. On 26 and 27 October alone, the 15th Sikhs lost three British and three Indian officers through injury, and among other ranks, eleven were killed, 240 were wounded and twelve went missing.[3] By 31 December 1914, the Indian Corps had suffered 9,579 casualties, including both British and Indian officers and privates, with 1,397 killed, 5,860 wounded and 2,322 missing: nearly one out of four sepoys who landed in Marseilles in late September and early October suffered some form of bodily injury or another.[4] By the end of 1915, the number had leapt to 28,800, including both British and Indians in the Indian Corps; a later count increased the figure to 34,252.[5] When the Indian infantry left for Mesopotamia in 1916, many of the regiments did not have any of their original men left.

Initially, the wounded Indians from the Western Front were sent to improvised hospitals in France. These included a hospital in a converted Jesuit college in Boulogne, large camps in Marseilles and Rouen, and at Château Mussot. There were also smaller hospitals, including a hotel overlooking the sea at Hardelot and a military academy at Montreuil that housed a large number of men from the Lahore Division wounded at Festubert. At the end of 1914, Lord Kitchener appointed Sir Walter Lawrence as the Commissioner for the Indian Sick and Wounded. Wanting to get the Indians quickly to 'warm and dry buildings', he had them moved to segregated hospitals spread across the south coast of England. In Brighton, the Royal Pavilion became the Dome and Pavilion Hospital, the Workhouse became the Kitchener Indian Hospital, and the York Place school was turned into the York Place Hospital; in the New Forest, there were the converted Lady Hardinge Indian Hospital and the Forest Park Hotel, also turned into a hospital, both at Brockenhurst; a convalescent home at Barton-on-Sea was converted and hospitals were also set up in Netley, Bournemouth and Milford-on-Sea. The level of medical care in these hospitals was high, in contrast to the nightmarish situation in the hospitals for Indians at the

One among the famous series of photographs of the Indian wounded recovering under the huge chandelier in the Dome of the Brighton Pavilion Hospital, taken by the well-known Brighton-based photographer A.H. Fry and the Canadian-born H.D. Girdwood for propaganda purposes.

---

[1] CIM, IOR, L/MIL/5/825/4.

[2] Ibid.

[3] Merewether and Smith, *The Indian Corps in France*, 49.

[4] Ibid., 199.

[5] Andrew Tait Jarboe, 'Soldiers of Empire: Indian Sepoys in and beyond the Imperial Metropole during the First World War, 1914–1918', PhD dissertation, Northeastern University, Boston, Massachusetts, submitted in April 2013, 182. Also see Samiksha Sehrawat, *Colonial Medical Care in North India: Gender, State and Society, c. 1840–1920* (Delhi, 2013), 187–248.

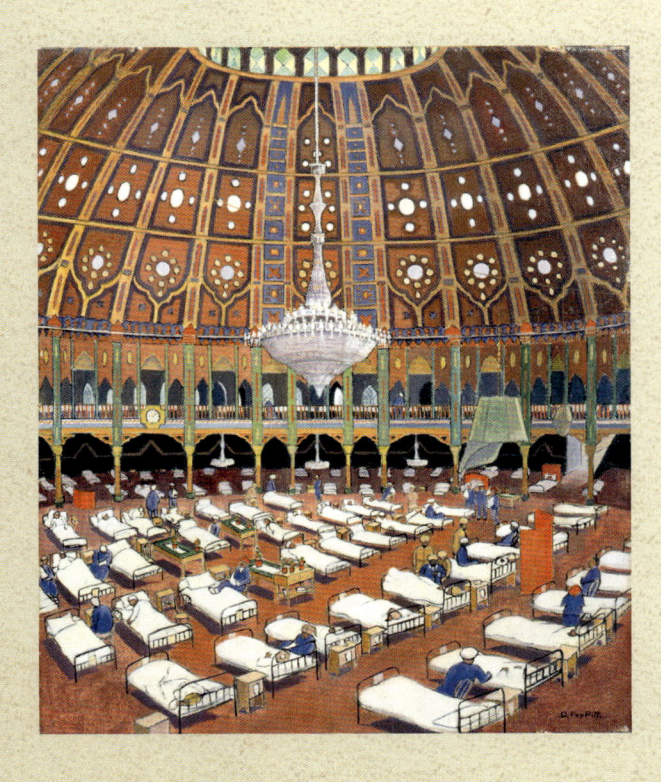

Douglas Fox-Pitt's celebrated 1919 oil painting of the Indian wounded recovering amidst the 'ornamentalism' of the Brighton Dome Room.

6 Letter dated 16 January 1915, CIM, IOR, L/MIL/5/825/1.

7 Letter of R.C. Volker, IOR, MSS Eur F 143/66, 14 October 1915.

8 Letter from the Viceroy to Sir Walter Lawrence, IOR, MSS Eur F143/73/26, 14 April 1915.

9 See Rozina Visram, *Asians in Britain*, 182–92.

10 Radhika Singha, 'Front Lines and Status Lines', 55.

11 Michèle Barrett, 'Death and the Afterlife: Britain's Colonies and Dominions', in S. Das, ed., *Race, Empire and First World War Writing*, 301–20.

other fronts, particularly in Mesopotamia where medical facilities were appalling and many were shipped to hospitals in Bombay.

Medical care, military strategy, imperial propaganda and racial anxiety were all fused and confused in these places; there was also a certain degree of goodwill towards these 'warriors from the East'. A classic example was the Dome and Pavilion Hospital, the most high-profile of these places: it treated some 2,000 men and was photographed, painted and even filmed. The Brighton Pavilion, the abandoned summer residence of George IV with its Indian facade and inner chinoiserie, was orientalism gone wild. It was hastily turned into a hospital for the Indians. Elaborate arrangements were made for food, sanitation and rituals, all sensitised to religious and caste rules: there were nine kitchens with caste cooks for each, three water taps for different religious groups in each ward and signs in Urdu, Hindi and Gurmukhi. An overwhelmed Sikh soldier applied a couplet from the wall of Diwan-i-Khas in Delhi to the Pavilion Hospital: 'If there be paradise on earth, it is this, it is this'.[6] This was the imperial mission richly realised: to overwhelm and dazzle the sepoy into loyalty. Every soldier, when leaving the Brighton Pavilion, was given a copy of the propaganda booklet *Indian Military Hospital: Royal Pavilion Brighton 1914–1915* – a short, illustrated history in 'English, Gurmuki and Urdu'. Photographs, postcards and lantern-slides of the wounded Indians recovering in the chandelier-hung Dome Room or idling on the lawns were widely circulated in India to create 'an impression of England's greatness, wealth and power'.[7] British imperialism beamed to the world with a seemingly 'philanthropic' face: the 'kindness' shown to the Indians was, for the Viceroy Lord Hardinge, of 'priceless value' for its political mileage and purposes of further recruitment in India.[8]

The other hospitals, though not as grand as the Pavilion, had similarly excellent medical facilities, particularly the Kitchener Indian Hospital. In addition to British doctors, the dressers and some doctors were often brought from India; British women nurses were allowed to work only in a supervisory capacity, aided by British and Indian male orderlies, after a racist fracas over a photograph of a sepoy with a nurse.[9] A crematorium was set up in Patcham near the Sussex Downs, and the Muslim sepoys were buried in Muslim Burial Ground at Woking. When the latrine sweeper 'Bigha' – an untouchable of a 'nominal' Muslim community – died and the imam refused to bury him, the vicar of Brockenhurst buried him in the churchyard of St Agnes Without.[10] This is in sharp contrast to thousands of sepoys who fell in Africa and Mesopotamia and for whom few gravestones exist.[11]

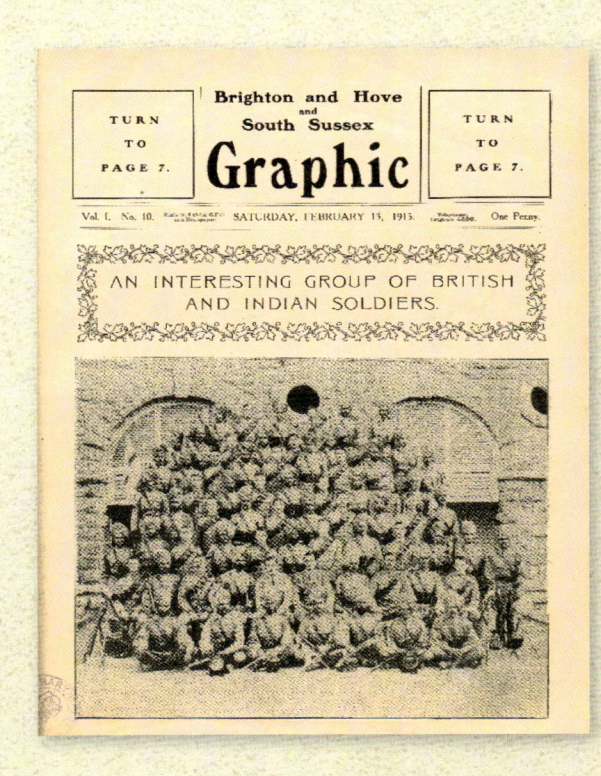

The sepoys' letters, many written from these hospitals, show gratitude at these measures, but two issues rankled. On 24 May 1915, in an anonymous letter addressed 'to the King', an aggrieved sepoy from a hospital at Milford-on-Sea wrote: 'The Indians have given their lives for eleven rupees. Any man who comes here wounded is returned thrice and four times to the trenches. Only that man goes to India who has lost an arm or a leg or an eye'.[12] The other issue was the sense of imprisonment. The British officials, fearful that the local presence of Indian troops may imperil 'white prestige' – particularly through potential liaisons with local women, fanning paranoid fantasies of sexual miscegenation – instituted a policy of segregation. High fences circled the Pavilion grounds, wires ran around the hospital at Barton-on-Sea and police guards were stationed at the Kitchener Indian Hospital. An Indian storekeeper at Barton bitterly complained: 'True, we are well-fed, and are given plenty of clothing; but the essential thing – freedom – is denied'.[13] However, the Indian wounded were sometimes taken on tours which they greatly enjoyed, under close British supervision, and musical and other entertainments were arranged; these images, in turn, were used for propaganda purposes.

The segregationist policy was particularly harsh, given the affection and warmth of the wounded Indians and the local people for each other. Apparently, the women in Brighton were so fond of the sepoys that some managed to circumvent surveillance, and walked arm in arm with the sepoys. Indeed, during their stay, the Indians became the talk of the town, endlessly reported, photographed, painted. J.N. Godbole, a sub-assistant surgeon and one of the most thoughtful and perceptive letter-writers, wrote of the local people: 'They talk pleasantly, treat us kindly and are pleased to see us. ... It is impossible to say why they become so bad on reaching India'.[14]

With the transfer of the Indian infantry to Mesopotamia in autumn 1915, the Indian hospitals closed down in early 1916. By then, they had treated 14,514 wounded Indians in all.

A copy of the *Brighton Graphic* (13 February 1915) showing British and Indian soldiers together.

Red Cross workers from India having a chat behind the firing lines.

12 CIM, IOR, L/MIL/5/825/3, 24 May 1915.

13 CIM, IOR, L/MIL/5/828/1, 2 December 1915.

14 CIM, IOR, L/MIL/5/825/2, 18 March 1915.

113

114

(Left) A wounded man is stretchered to the regimental aid post. (Above left) An injured soldier is being lifted to the ambulance. (Above right) Stretcher-bearers carry a wounded soldier over a gangway while two sepoys, wearing gasmasks and brandishing their weapons, pose in the trenches. All three stereoscopic images were part of a large collection of photographs taken at Fauquissart – the signpost is visible in the photograph on the extreme right – by H.D. Girdwood and used for propaganda purposes during his lecture tours throughout India.

MILITAIRE PRÉPARATOIRE D'INFANTERIE
CASERNE DUVAL
LAHORE INDIAN
GENERAL HOSPITAL
NO ADMISSION
DÉFENSE D'ENTRER

(Left) The military school at Montreuil was converted into a hospital for the Indian wounded, particularly for men from the Lahore Division.

(Above) Convalescent Indian soldiers, resting in front of the ramparts of Montreuil-sur-Mer, chat with local children.

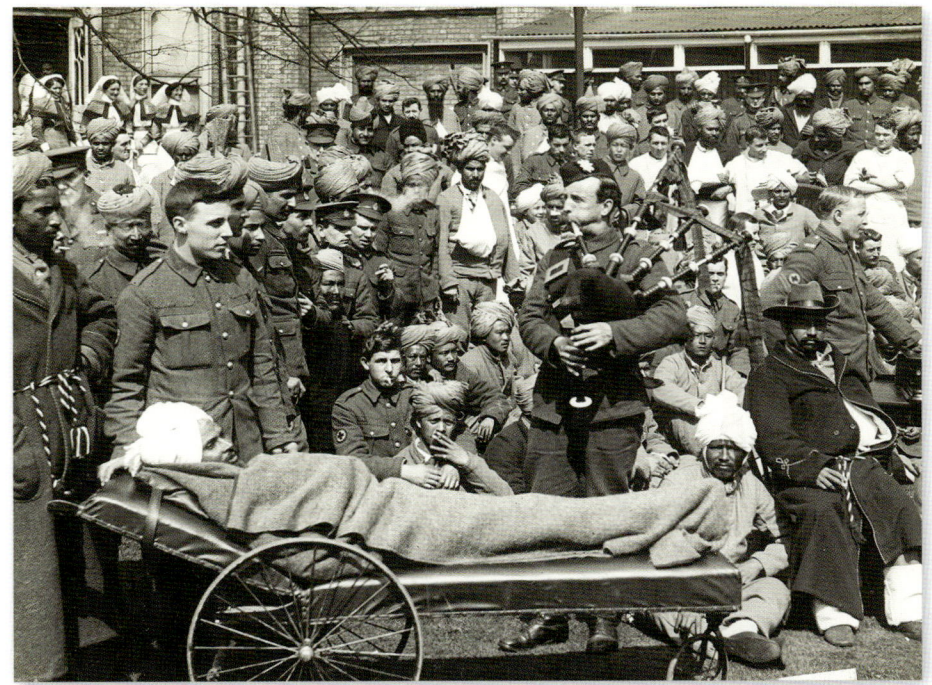

The sepoys relax on the grounds of the Brighton Dome and Pavilion Hospital, framed by trees; the high fence that shut in the sepoys and prevented them from going to town is nowhere to be seen. The photograph was taken by A.H. Fry and published in *Indian Military Hospital: Royal Pavilion Brighton 1914–1915* with the caption 'In the Gardens, Dome in Background'. The photograph below, taken by H.D. Girdwood, was accompanied by the caption: 'The wounded listening to the bagpipe and sunning themselves'. In both, the Indian wounded are woven into a visual narrative of upper-class British leisure with pastoral overtones, calculated to create the maximum 'political impression' in Britain, India and beyond.

This staged but tender picture, taken by H.D. Girdwood on the lawns of the Brighton Pavilion, shows a wounded sepoy on a wheelchair dictating a letter to a fellow sepoy or scribe. It gives insights into the process of composition of these letters. The sepoy lightly leans across to touch the scribe in a gesture of gratitude, intimacy and affection, in sharp contrast to the brisk, anonymous brush of fingers of his fellow non-literate sepoy with the paymaster on p. 36 as he collects his pay.

Four Sikh officers in their room, symmetrically arranged, the whiteness of their turbans blending with the white linen and walls, while the open door, carefully framed, suggests mobility and freedom – things that were often denied to these men. The level of medical care and sensitivity to issues of caste and ethnicity were however excellent.

Wounded Indians pose with British officers and female nurses at the Corn Exchange, Brighton. In most hospitals, the official rule was that British women nurses would be employed only in a supervisory capacity while male orderlies did the actual nursing after a fracas over an innocuous photograph of a female British nurse with an Indian patient.

122

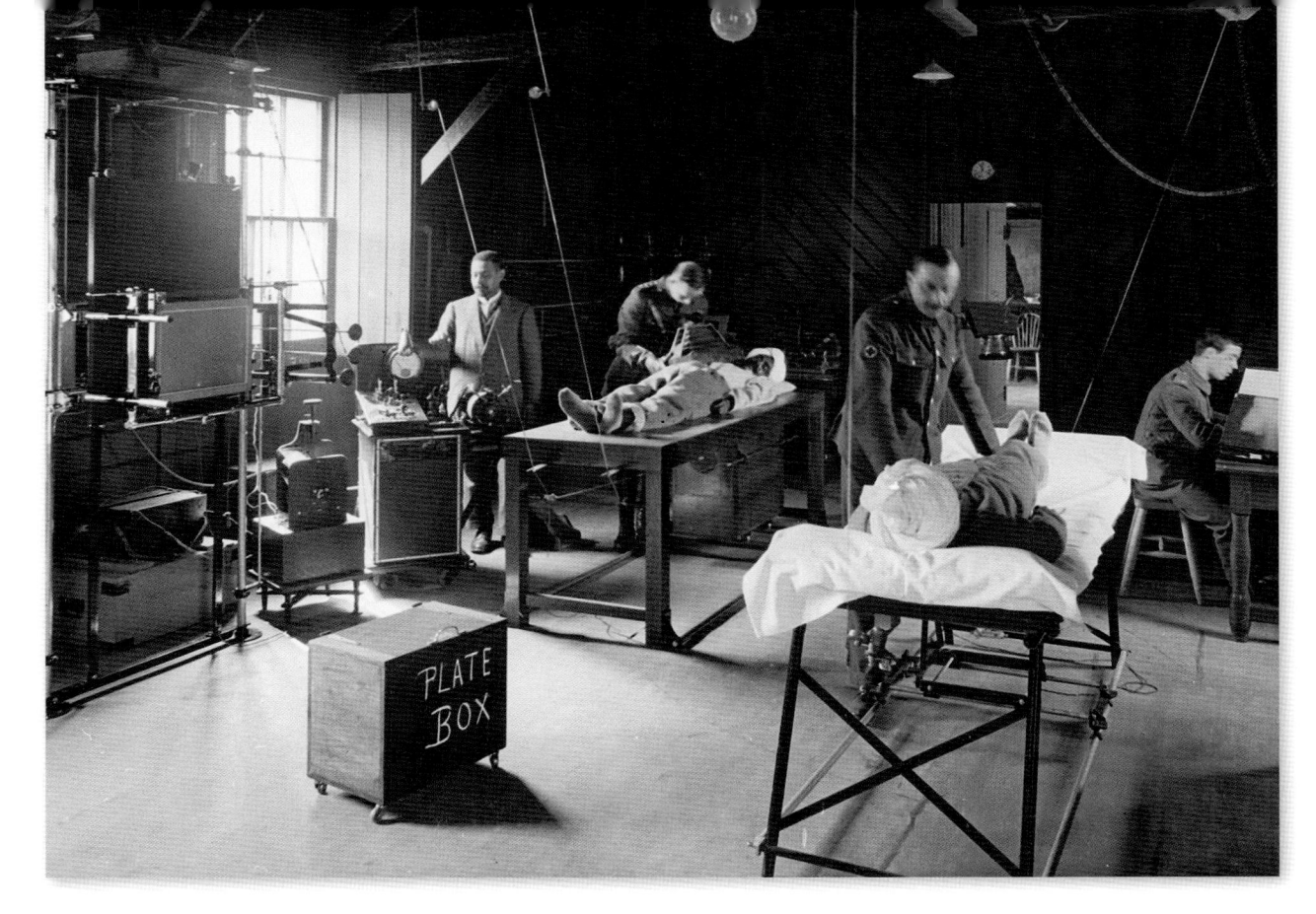

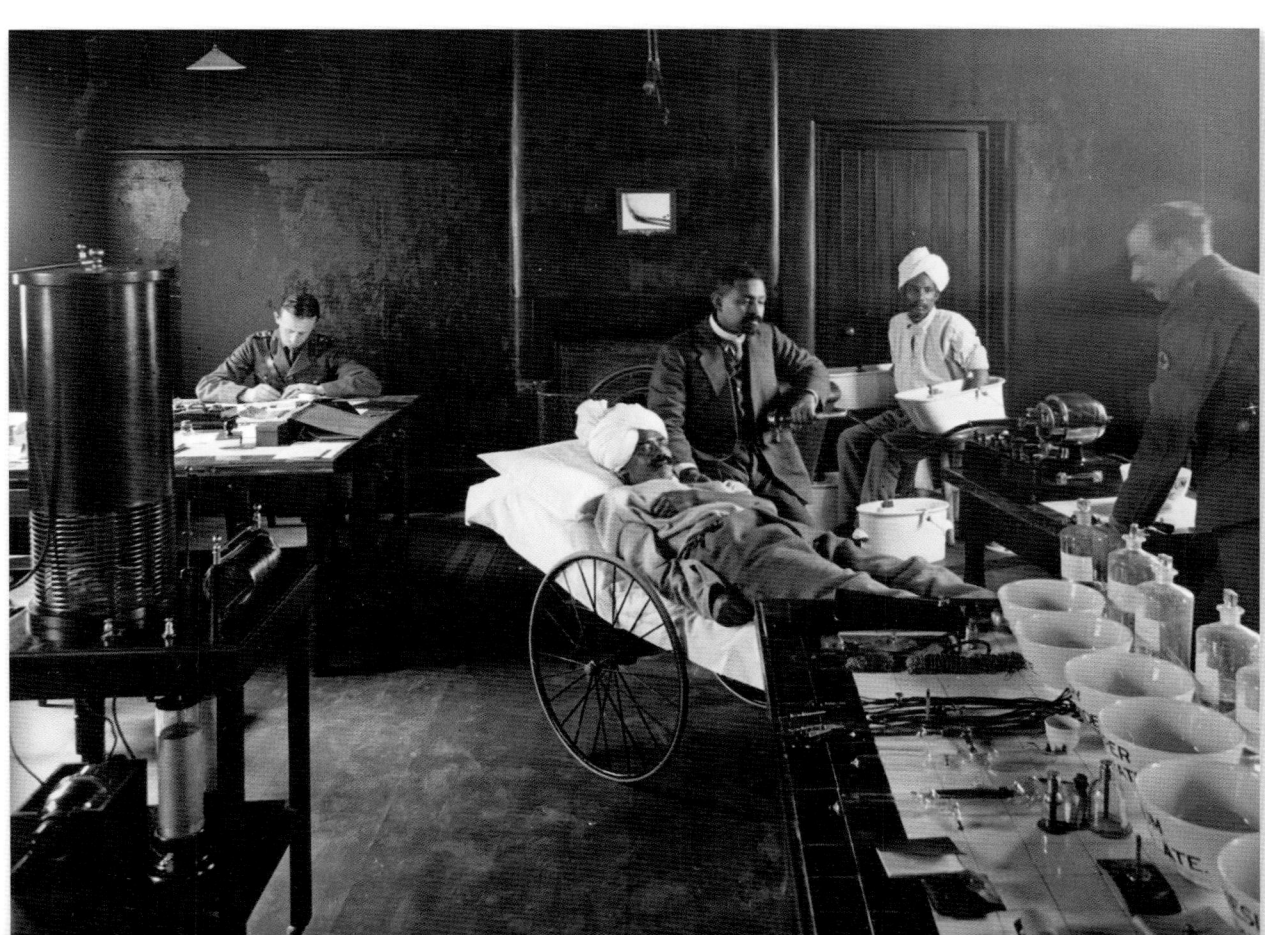

All three photographs are from the Kitchener Indian Hospital in Brighton. The top image (left) shows the X-ray room at the Kitchener Hospital while the one below shows the electrical and galvanic treatment room. In the second picture, the sepoy seated near the door is receiving galvanic treatment while the one in the bed is undergoing electrical treatment. The Kitchener Hospital admitted some 3,890 patients, only twenty-six of whom died. It had some of the most advanced medical facilities of the day but it was relentlessly used for propaganda purposes, evident in the contemporary captions that accompanied these images: 'Modern science is being utilized to the greatest possible extent in relieving the sufferings of our Indian wounded' or 'Every scientific help is being employed to relieve the sufferings of our Indian wounded'. (Above) Sombre-faced Indian officers are seen on parade in the hospital grounds. All three were taken by H.D. Girdwood who went on an extended lecture tour in India, promoting his photographs and film *With the Empire's Fighters*.

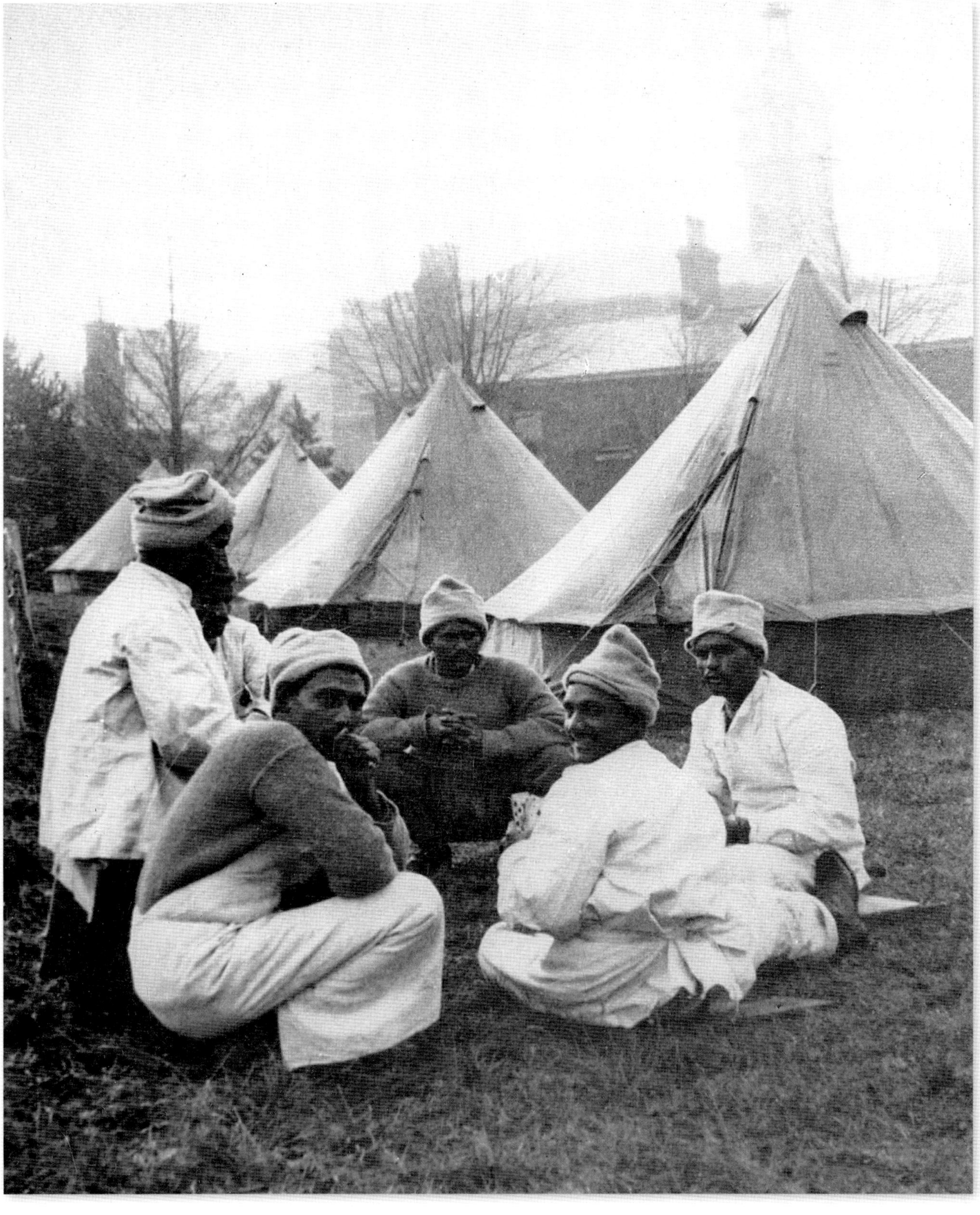

(Left) Indian sepoys outside some makeshift tents at the Lady Hardinge Hospital. Soldiers in this hospital complained bitterly about the cold.

The Mont Dore was one of the most exclusive hotels in Bournemouth and was converted into a hospital for the Indian war wounded.

(Above right) The Indians pose before they are taken for a motor car ride to produce an image of wartime Indo-British comradeship – though one wonders what the Indian soldier, reaching across the car, is up to.

(Below right) Indians take a stroll down the beach, watched by openly curious women and children. J.N. Godbole, a sub-assistant surgeon at Bournemouth General Hospital, wrote on 18 March 1915 to a friend in Pune: 'The people here are of a very amiable disposition. ... We do not hear the words "damn" and "bloody" at all frequently, as in India ... The people here are charming. It is impossible to say why they become so bad on reaching India.'

Convalescent Indian sepoys enjoy a performance in Hampshire. At Brockenhurst, the Lady Hardinge Hospital, and two minor sections, the former Balmer Lawn and Forest Park hotels, provided around 640 beds. The hospital became so overcrowded that occasionally the Indian wounded had to be accommodated on mattresses on the floor. Overcrowding seems to have been a problem even when it came to entertainment. (Above) Both British and Indian audience watch a performance, while the unlucky ones peep in through the window (below). (Right) The lucky sepoy, smiling broadly, speaks to a sari-clad Miss Gakarjan – presumably one of the performers – while the others look on. A young sepoy, just behind him, looks straight into the camera.

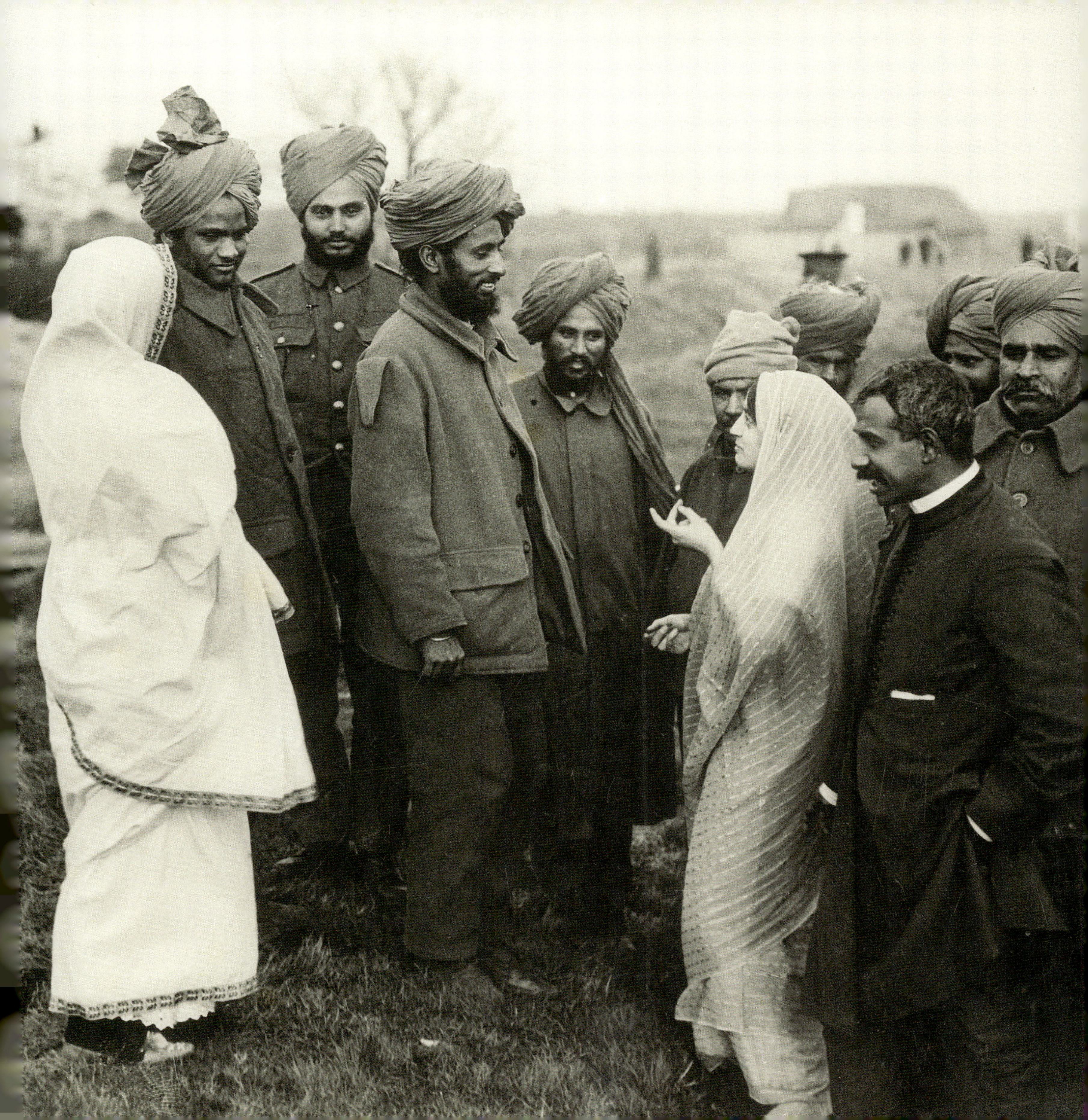

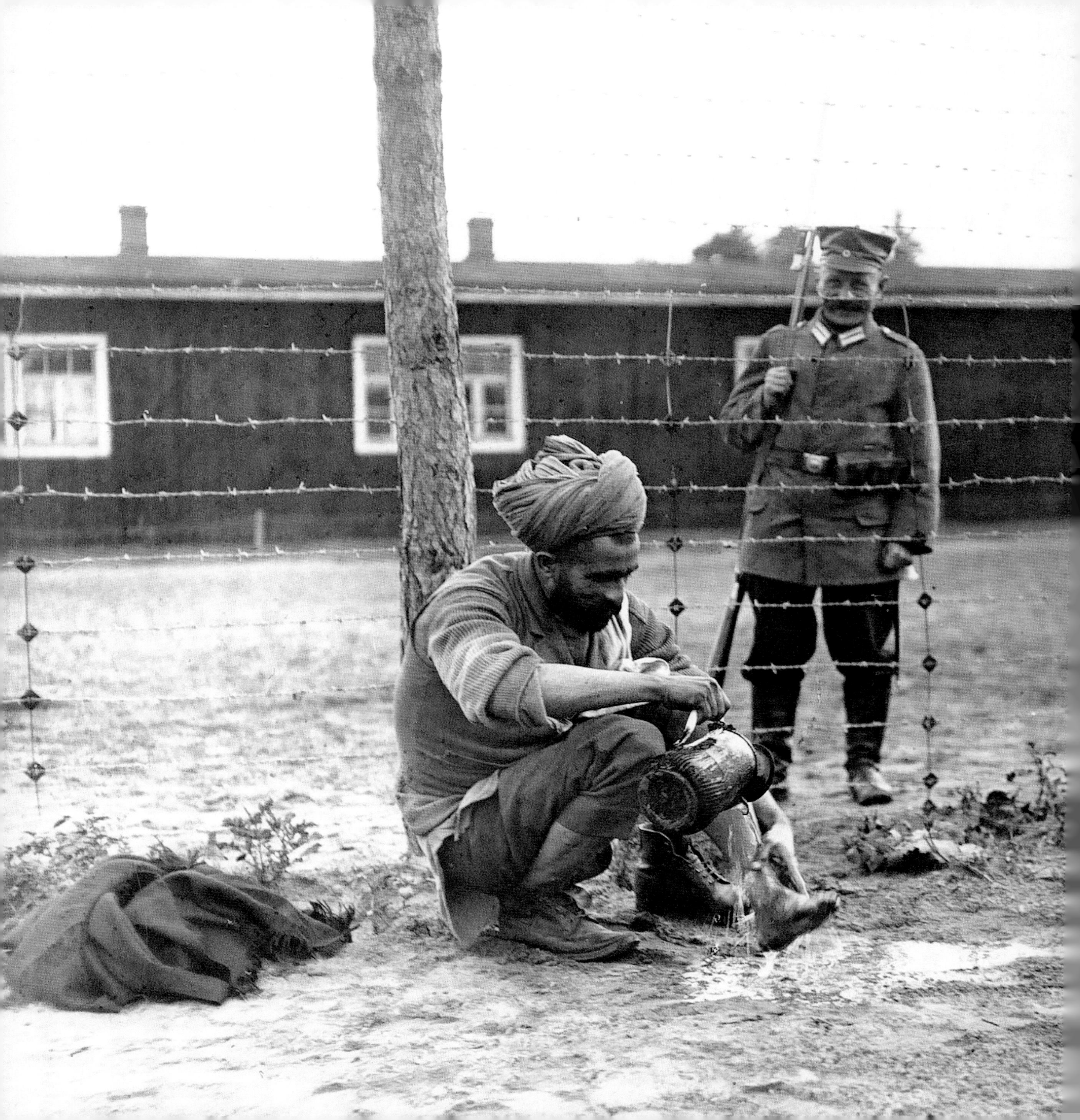

Prisoners

On 11 December 1916, Mall Singh, a prisoner-of-war (POW) in Wünsdorf in Germany, spoke the following words into the funnel of a phonograph machine:

> There was a man who would have butter back in India
> He would also have two sers of milk.
> He served for the British.
> He joined the European War.
> He was captured by the Germans.
> He wants to go back to India.
> If he goes back to India then he will get that same food.[1]

We can hear his voice even today from an old shellac recording preserved in the sound archives of the Humboldt University in Berlin. Mall Singh's testimony was among the 2,677 audio recordings done by the Royal Prussian Phonographic Commission, between 29 December 1915 and 19 December 1918, of the First World War POWs held in Germany, including a large number of non-white colonial prisoners. Singh's voice is wistful, chant-like and poignant; it is interrupted by awkward pauses, sharp intakes of breath and the constant scratch of the phonograph disc. He refers to himself in the third person, as if he is already dead. We do not know whether Singh lived to go back to his native land, or died in captivity.

Around a thousand Indian soldiers were taken as prisoners-of-war in Europe; the number was far higher in Mesopotamia, where almost 10,000 Indians were made prisoners and subjected to sustained Turkish brutality.[2] The Indians captured on the Western Front were taken to various POW camps but later grouped together at the twin camps of Zossen (Weinberglager) and Wünsdorf (Halbmondlager or Halfmoon Camp), south of Berlin. The camps were built towards the end of 1914. In spring 1917, they were moved to a camp in Morile-Marculesti in occupied southern Romania and then repatriated at the end of the war. Photographic evidence suggests that there were also a few Indian prisoners in other camps, such as Friedrichsfeld in Germany, Leysin in Switzerland and Schneidemühl near Posen in today's Poland. Not much is known about the Indians in these other camps.

The main POW camps for the Indians in Europe were the twin sites in Zossen and Wünsdorf.[3] These camps held a large number of colonial prisoners of African, Tatar, Georgian or South Asian origin. However, within Wünsdorf, a separate camp – the 'Inderlager' (the Indian Camp) – was created, where Indians were segregated from the other colonial troops.

In addition to these 1,000 Indians captured on the Western Front, there were around 860 Indian civilians –

Ram Singh, an Indian POW, washes his feet before praying while a German guard looks on. This intimate detail stands out against the desolation of the landscape and the barbed wire separating the two.

[1] Mall Singh's voice recording is among the 1,650 shellac recordings held at the sound archives of the Humboldt University. The text is translated by Arshdeep Brar. Refer to Philip Scheffner's film *The Halfmoon Files* (2007) and Santanu Das, 'The Singing Subaltern', *Parallax* 17:3 (2011), 4–18.

[2] Heike Liebau, 'South Asian Prisoners of War' (www.1914-1918-online.de); and Heather Jones, 'Colonial Prisoners in Germany and the Ottoman Empire', in *Race, Empire and First World War Writing*.

[3] See the brilliant collection 'When the War Began, We Heard of Several Kings' and accompanying CD. I am deeply grateful to Heike Liebau and Britta Lange for guiding me to the materials in German archives. Also see Gerhard Höpp, *Muslime in der Mark* (1997); and Margot Kahleyss, *Muslime in Brandenburg* (1998).

Cover of the propaganda book *Unsere Feinde (Our Enemies)* by camp commander Otto Stiehl (1916).

Two lithograph portraits of Indian POWs by the Jewish artist Hermann Struck which were used as part of ethnological research.

[4] Franziska Roy, 'South Asian Civilian Prisoners of War in First World War Germany', in Roy, Liebau and Ahuja, *'When the War Began'*, 53–95.

[5] Extensive documents are to be found in various archives in Berlin, particularly Politisches Archiv des Auswärtigen Amtes and Archiv der Brandenburgischen Akademie der Wissenschaften. Also see Britta Lange's important articles 'South Asian Soldiers and German Academics', in Roy, Liebau and Ahuja, *When the War Began*, 149–84 and 'Academic Research on (Coloured) Prisoners of War', in Dominiek Dendooven and Piet Chielens, *World War I: Five Continents in Flanders* (Ypres, 2008), 153–65.

particularly businessmen, students and *lascars* (seamen) – who were detained in various camps but brought to Wünsdorf in 1917.[4] The Wünsdorf camp was singular in two respects: it was a showcase, propaganda camp where the Indians were subjected to sustained anti-British propaganda; it also became a site for serious ethnological research. Propaganda, ethnology and linguistic study went hand in hand.[5] The curious fallout today is that the Wünsdorf camp has the 'perfect' archive, with photographs, sketches, paintings, voice recordings and even film-clippings which help us to reconstruct the inmates' lives.

During the war years, the German Foreign Office opened a special bureau – Nachrichtenstelle für den Orient (NfO) – to co-ordinate their propaganda. Its aim was to deluge the 'Oriental' prisoners with propaganda leaflets, lectures and newspapers and try to whip up a religious *jihad*. Wünsdorf and Zossen soon became centres of propaganda: a mosque was built and religious practices encouraged; a special camp newspaper *El Jihad* was produced in different languages and the Indian version, published in Urdu and Hindi, was renamed *Hindostan*. Indian nationalists from the Indian Independence Committee (IIC) in Berlin were invited to give lectures to the prisoners and infuse them with anti-colonial and *jihadist* sentiments. Men of the IIC included highly educated nationalists and Marxists such as Virendranath Chattopadhyaya and Tarak Nath Das. In early 1915, even an expedition via Turkey to Kabul was launched by the IIC: it was led by the German diplomat Werner Otto von Hentig and included six Indian POWs. The mission was ultimately unsuccessful.

Closely allied was the work of the Royal Prussian Phonographic Commission. Even if the famous German anthropologist Leo Frobenius published his pamphlet 'The People's Circus of Our Enemies', the presence of colonial prisoners on German soil sparked widespread interest. Masterminded by the philologist Wilhelm Doegen, the commission comprised thirty academics – including linguists, musicologists and philologists – who toured thirty-one prison camps in wartime Germany and made 2,677 recordings.[6] Of these, around 300 are recordings of stories, songs and testimonies in Indian languages, such as Hindi, Urdu, Punjabi, Bengali, Nepali, Baluchi and Garhwali – many of them recorded by Heinrich Lüders, a professor at the Oriental Seminar of Berlin University. The men were often asked to stand in front of a phonograph and told to read a text, recite a poem or sing a song. Mall Singh was one of them. Alongside these recordings, palatograms were made to determine tongue position and pronunciation. The presence of colonial prisoners led to ethnological research by Felix von Luschan, an academic and curator of the Berlin Ethnological Museum: the men were measured and photographs were taken from the front and back, in order to 'race' them. About fifty of these portrait photographs still exist. Meanwhile, a series of portraits was painted by the German Jewish artist Hermann Struck, some signed by the men themselves.

How did the Germans and the Indians perceive each other, and were there any cultural encounters? Otto Stiehl, the commander of the camp at Wünsdorf, was a keen photographer and his albums provide tantalising insights into daily life in the camp. In 1916 he published a book with the title *Unsere Feinde: 96 Charakterköpfe aus deutschen Kriegsgefangenenlagern* and, a few years later, Wilhelm Doegen published his research as *Unter fremden Völkern: Eine neue Völkerkunde* (1925). How did the Indians feel and experience captivity? Conditions seem to have been rather grim, with a death-rate of 16.8% among Indians.[7] Some sports and religious festivals appear to have been organised, though men complained of the cold and the poor food. The sound-recordings remain the most haunting testimonies of these men. One of the most moving lyrics was composed and sung by Jasbahadur Rai, a 26-year-old Gurkha POW, a few months before his death. It was recorded on 6 June 1916 at 4pm at Wünsdorf:

I don't want to stay in a European country, please send me to India
Surviving brings no progress, dying brings no knowledge,
Bodies must go, and when mine goes, if you wash it, how much can it be washed?
Fire of straw, my body has become like a string, if I cry, how much can I cry?[8]

A religious painting done by an Indian POW in the Wünsdorf camp (Museum of European Culture, Berlin).

Painting of Gurkha POWs by the German artist Thomas Baumgartner in 1916, as reproduced in *Deutschlands Gegner in Weltkriege* (Germany's Opponents in the World War), c. 1919

6 See Wilhelm Doegen, *Unter fremden Völkern: eine neue Völkerkunde* (Berlin, 1925). Also see Lange, 'South Asian Soldiers'; and Santanu Das, 'Indian Sepoy Experience in Europe, 1914–1918: Archive, Language and Feeling', *Twentieth Century British History*, 25, 2014, 391–417.

7 Höpp, *Muslime in der Mark*, 50.

8 Jasbahadur Rai from Sikkim/Darjeeling, 'Gurkha Song, Own Words', Lautarchiv, Humboldt University, Berlin, PK 307. I am very grateful to Dr Anne Stirr for transcribing and translating the song.

A group of Indian prisoners are lined up, waiting to be transferred to a POW camp in Germany. Mohammed Hossin, a captured lascar in the Wünsdorf camp, remembers a poignant detail about the transfer of POWs: 'He [the chief] asked how were doing in the camp. [We said] we want to go back to India. He misunderstood this and sent us to the Indian prison camp.'

(Above) Two turbaned Indians, seated next to the nursing sister, as well as one seated on the ground to the extreme left on the front row are seen along with the British, French and Russian internees at the POW camp at Leysin. According to the recommendation of the International Committee of the Red Cross, an agreement was signed between France, Germany, Britain, Belgium and Russia about the repatriation of seriously sick or wounded POWs through Switzerland. A number of sick or wounded POWs were also interned in Switzerland, totalling around 68,000 at the end of the war. The first British POWs – some 300 officers and other ranks – arrived in Switzerland on 31 May 1916 and were then joined by another 400: they were mostly interned in south-western Switzerland, east of Lake Geneva. Leysin was used for POWs suffering from tuberculosis.
(Bottom) Two Gurkha riflemen at Schneidemühl camp near Posen. The staged appearance and the soft focus give the impression more of a studio-piece than a prisoner-of-war camp picture: neither the photographer nor the exact circumstances of this tantalising photograph are known.

The Halbmondlager (Halfmoon Camp) at Wünsdorf near Berlin in all its vastness and desolation. It housed a substantial number of prisoners, including POWs from South Asia, Africa and the Middle East. This propaganda camp, primarily for Muslim POWs, was built towards the end of 1914, and the mosque, dominating the site, was erected in 1915. This was the first mosque on German soil. A contemporary record describes the building: 'The vertically rising exterior surfaces of the cupola were realised in an ivory colour, the remaining surfaces in stripes of red and grey.' Photographs of life at the Halfmoon Camp and its twin the Weinberg Camp at Zossen have come to us through 136 glass slides and glass-plate negatives, found by Margot Kahleyss in 1980s in the then European section of Berlin Ethnological Museum. This collection was supplemented by another 232 glass-plate negatives from the archive of the Berlin Society of Anthropology, Ethnology and Prehistory.

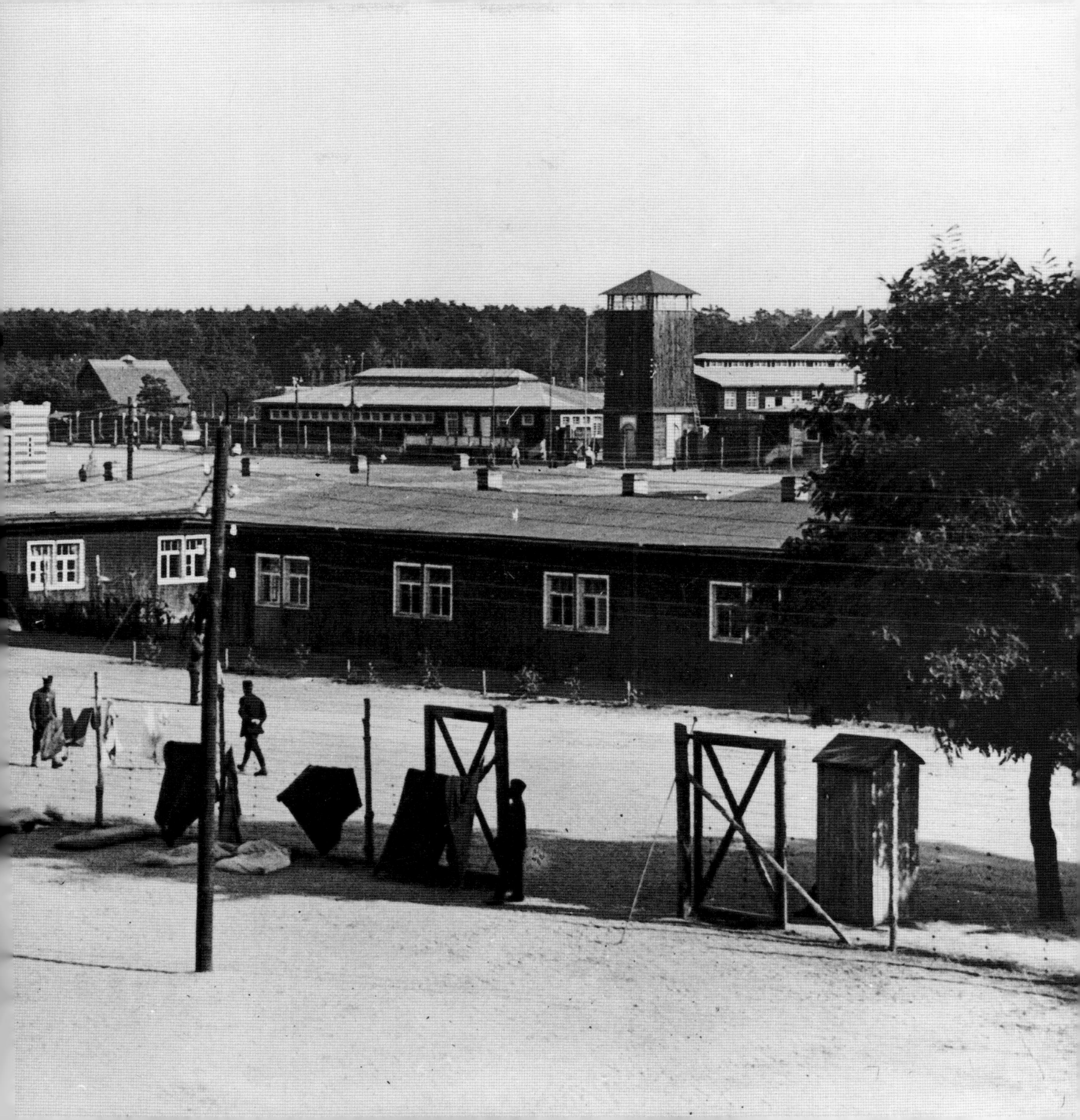

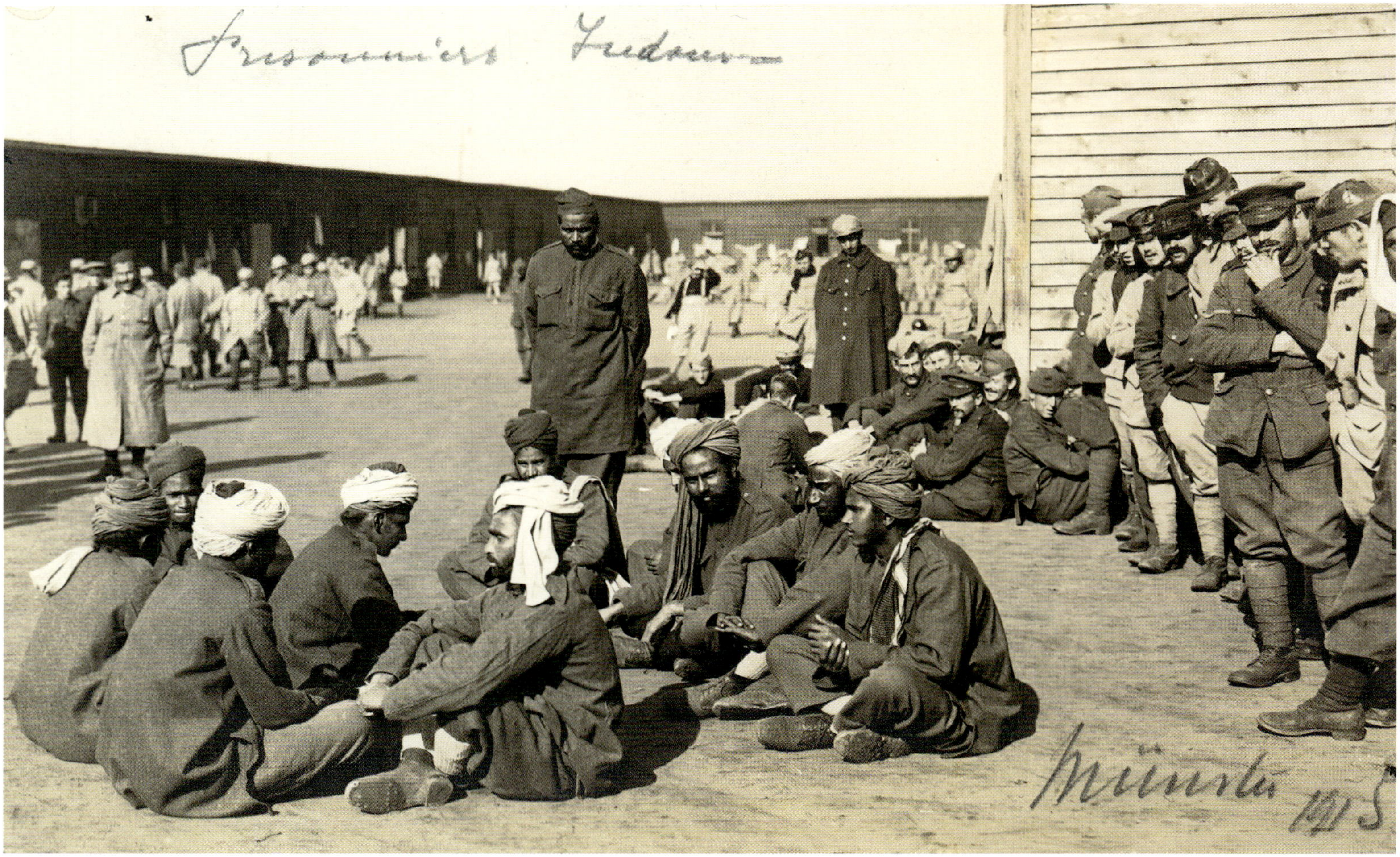
Prisonniers Indous
Münster 1915

Both photographs show the daily life of South Asian prisoners at the Halfmoon Camp. Official 'cinematographic and photographic pictures' of everyday camp life were taken by professional photographers and used as propaganda images; these are often stilted. The private photographs of Otto Stiehl are more natural, showing the men engaged in the daily round of activities. The above pictures capture these men, well-clothed and relaxed, in outdoor spaces. However, many suffered bitterly from the cold, and the rate of mortality among the South Asian prisoners was high. A large number died from ailments such as tuberculosis, typhoid and respiratory problems.

Cultural and religious festivals were encouraged and organised in the camp. Otto Stiehl took this photograph of what he referred to as an 'Indian Spring Feast' in February 1917. What exactly was enacted is not known but the painted faces, false beards and the moustached man in a sari (second on the left) suggest a degree of creativity, festivity and good cheer. Similarly, 'Dusserha' (a Hindu autumn festival celebrating the triumph of good over evil) was performed at the Wünsdorf camp. Such moments would have served as a strong, nostalgic link to their lives in India. The POWs suffered from intense homesickness. Mohammed Hossin, a Bengali *lascar* (seaman), who stayed in the Wünsdorf camp till the end of the war, referred to it as *'garod'* (asylum) and pleaded on the phonograph to be allowed to return home: though admittedly well fed, 'we want to go back to India.' [author's translation]

139

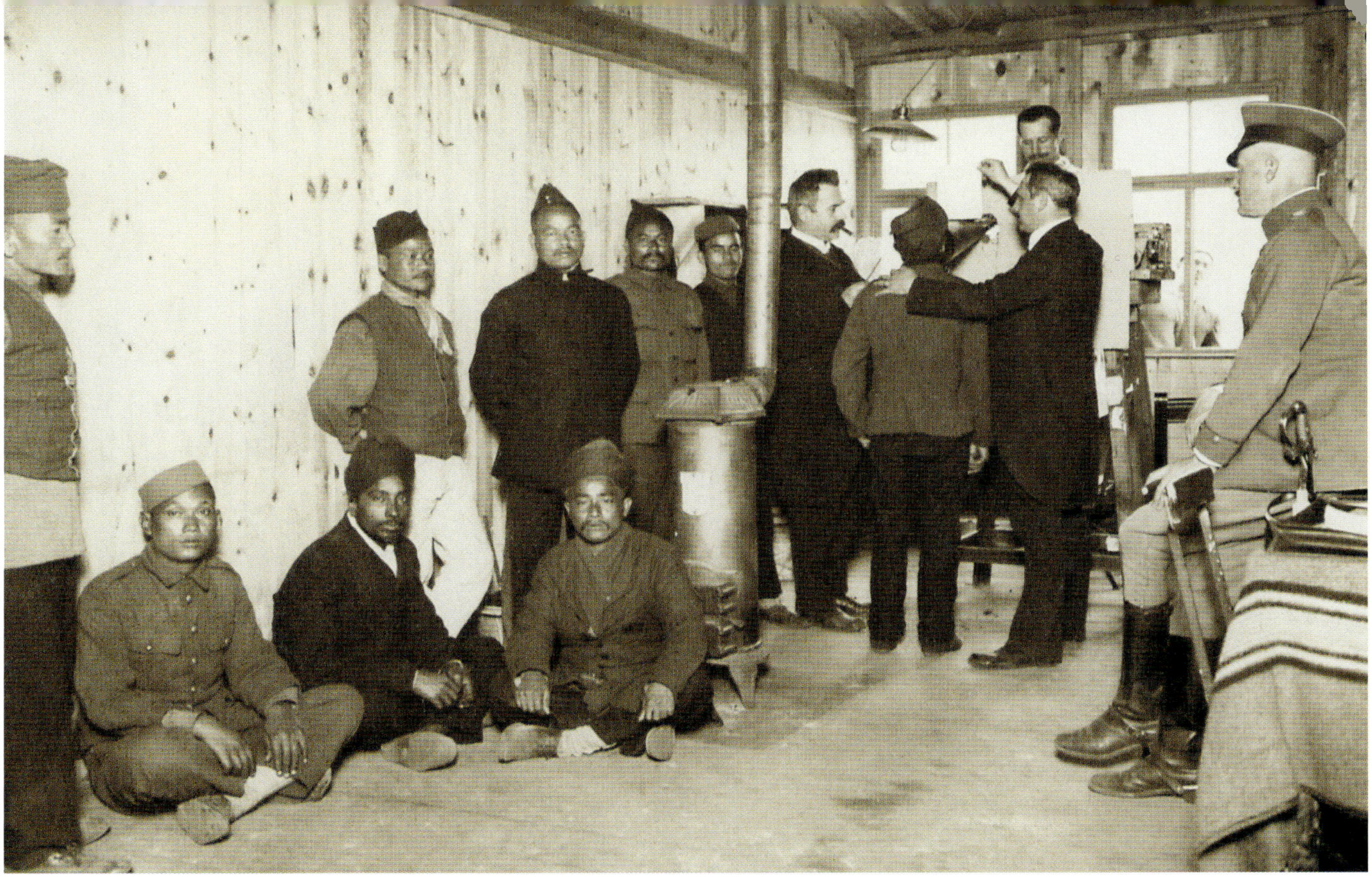

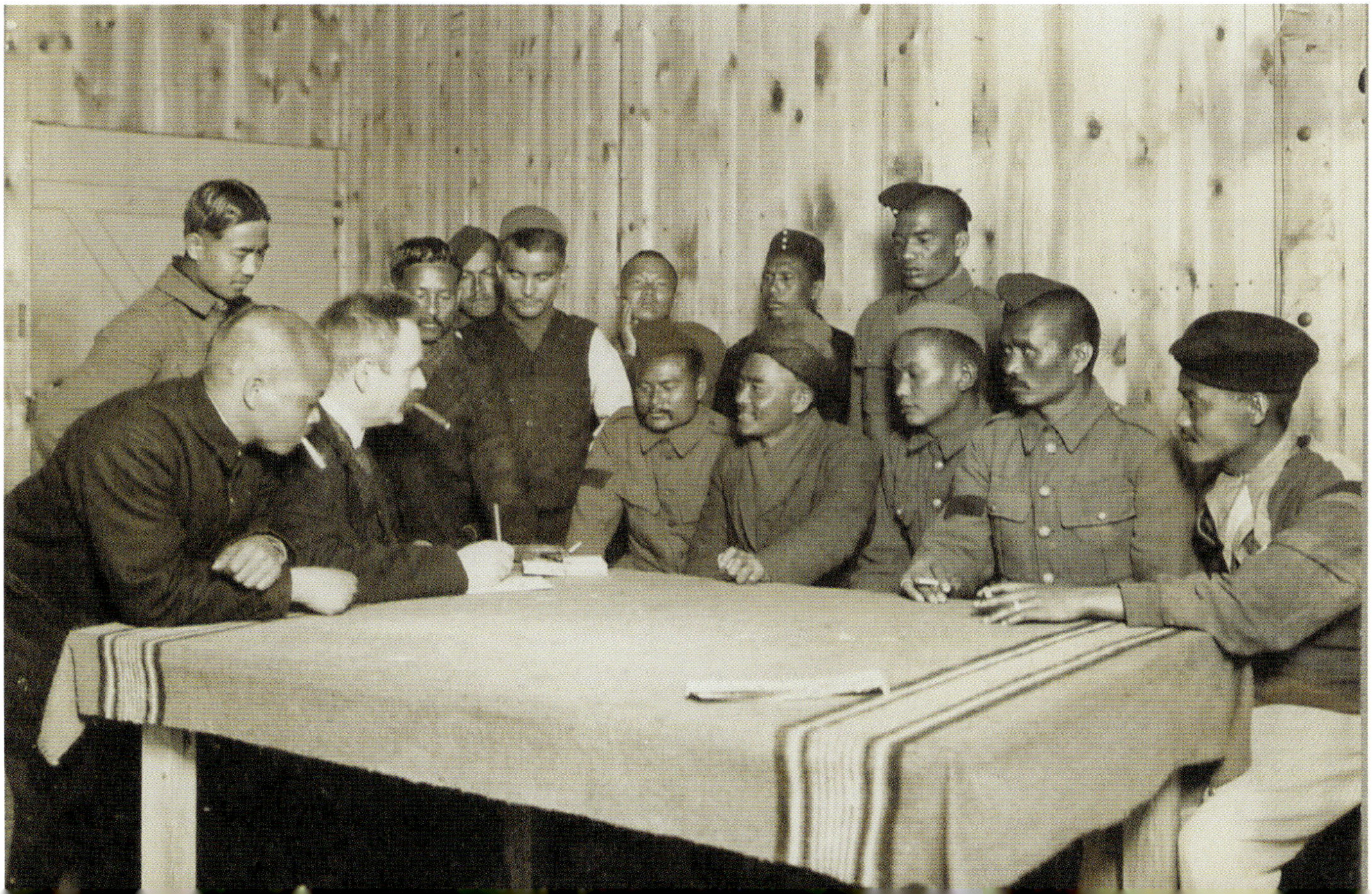

(Left, above) The photograph shows an audio recording session taking place as part of the project of the Royal Prussian Phonographic Commission headed by Wilhelm Doegen. Flanked by German officials and academics, a sepoy is reading from a page held in front of him while others look into the camera. Some of these handwritten texts have survived. Some of the POWs sang songs, played music or related an anecdote.

(Left, below) Of all the German academics, Professor Heinrich Lüders perhaps had the closest contact with the Indian POWs. As professor at the Oriental Seminar of Berlin University, he was the main person responsible for research on Indian languages within the context of the Prussian Phonographic Commission. Here, he is seen with a group of Gurkha sepoys, taking down notes on Gurung in the Wünsdorf camp.

(Right) This photograph was taken by Otto Stiehl and published in his 1916 propaganda book *Unsere Feinde* as 'Indian, Rajput. Sultan Singh, Mhow'. The Wünsdorf camp became a 'colonial laboratory' where these portrait photographs were taken; these were aligned to the work of physical anthropologists who took body measurements of the prisoners in order to determine 'racial elements' from their physical features. The anthropologist Von Eickstedt conducted research on seventy-six Sikhs from northern Punjab.

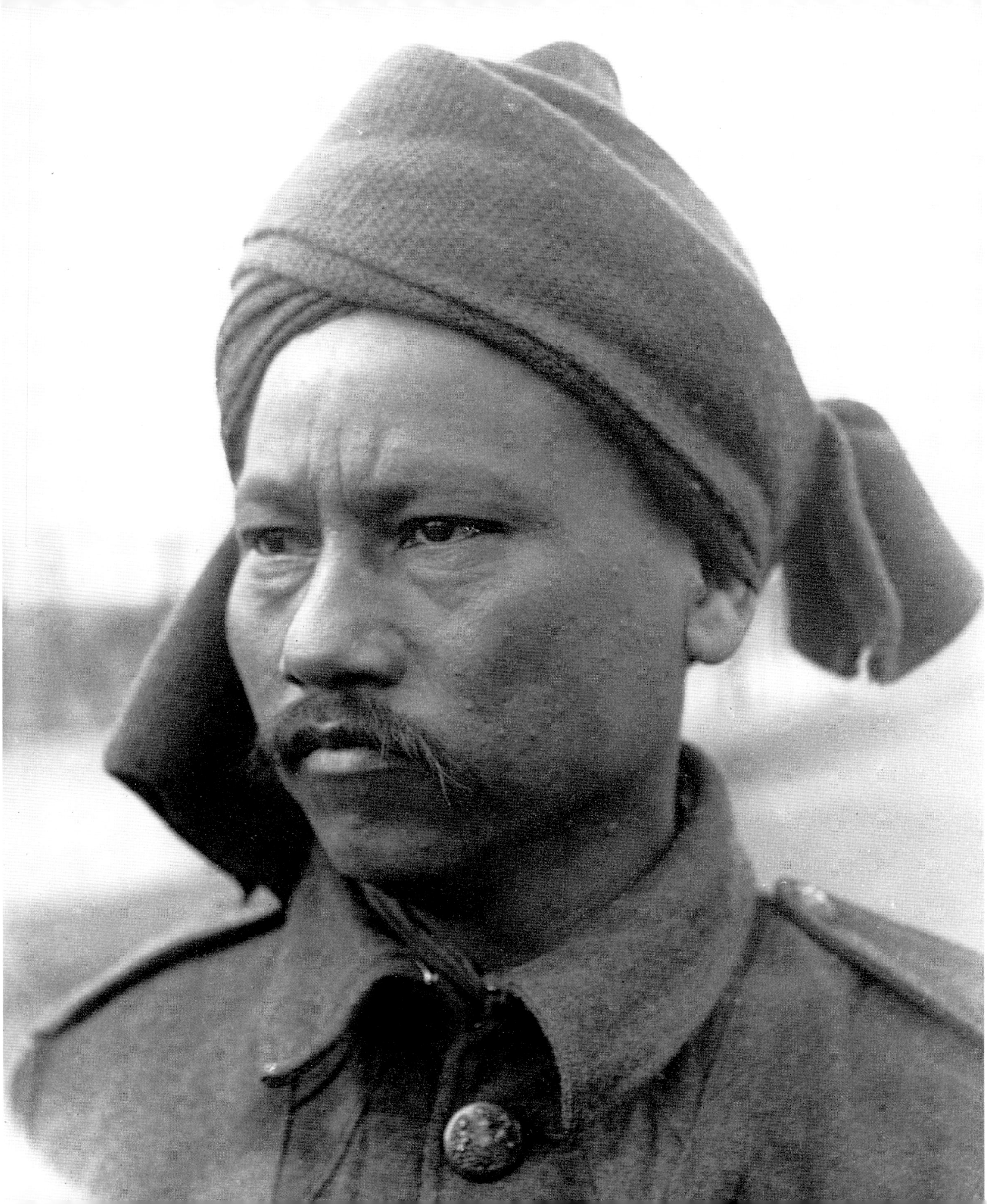

(Left) Another photograph from Otto Stiehl's, *Unsere Feinde* with the title: 'Gurkha. Serg. Ganga Ram, Dharmsala. District Kangra'. There is a four-minute-long voice recording from Ganga Ram where he narrates the 'Story of the Prodigal Son' in English. (Above) A photograph showing three Indian prisoners of war and signed 'Indes Anglaises'. Photographs are one of our main sources to understand life at the POW camps in Germany but as Margaret Kahleyss, who found many of the original glass-slides notes, the question remains: what was *not* photographed?

Afterword

At the time of writing *The Indian Corps in France* (1918), Lieutenant-Colonel Merewether and Sir Frederick Smith felt that the 'present struggle' had been waged on so immense a scale that many units had failed to receive 'contemporary justice', but 'perhaps none more conspicuously than those of the Indian Army Corps'.[1]

In the immediate post-war years, attempts were made to rectify this, not only in words but through acts and in stone. On 19 July 1919, the Indian troops took part in the Victory March and Peace Pageant to the Cenotaph in London. Two years later, in Delhi, in 1921, the Duke of Connaught laid the foundation stone for the All India War Memorial (now known as the India Gate) designed by Edwin Lutyens, which was inaugurated formally on 12 February 1931. It is dedicated to the Indian dead of the First World War as well as those killed in the third Anglo-Afghan War – with the names of both groups etched on its walls – showing how the two conflicts bled into each other in the country's memory. Today, the India Gate has been so seamlessly assimilated into the post-independence history of India and evolved into a nationalist icon – with the Amar Jayan Jyoti or eternal flame burning at its base to commemorate the Indo-Pakistan War of 1971 – that few remember that it was originally an imperial war monument. Indeed, was Lutyens's monument an ode to the empire or to the Indians who died? And for whom or what did they fight? Speaking with a forked tongue, the monument is almost emblematic of the palimpsestic nature of First World War memory in India: at once present and absent, imperial and national.

Similarly in 1921, in Britain, was erected the dome-like *chattri* (meaning umbrella or pavilion) Memorial, perched high on the South Downs in Sussex and buffeted by the wind and the clouds. It commemorates the fifty-three Sikh and Hindu sepoys who were nursed in Brighton and were cremated there. Today, it is the site of the Chattri Memorial Group – a diverse and multiracial group of people, dedicated to perpetuating the memory of these men, and they hold an annual service there. On 26 September 2010, a memorial tablet bearing all the fifty-three names was unveiled by the Commonwealth War Graves Commission (CWGC).[2] Of the Muslim sepoys, nineteen were

[1] Merewether and Smith, *The Indian Corps in France*, xvi–xvii.

[2] See the website www.chattri.org/.

buried at the Muslim Burial Ground at Woking, but, following disrepair and vandalism, the bodies were removed to the Brockwood Military Cemetery in Surrey by the Commonwealth War Graves Commission in 1968. The Burial Ground has recently been renovated.

Perhaps the most haunting of the monuments is the Neuve-Chapelle War Memorial designed by Sir Herbert Baker and unveiled by the Earl of Birkenhead on 7 October 1927.[3] The ceremony was attended by the Maharajah of Kapurthala, Marshal Ferdinand Foch, Rudyard Kipling and a large contingent of Indian veterans. The memorial incorporates both British and Indian motifs. At the centre stands a fifteen-foot-high column, with a lotus capital, the Star of India and the imperial crown, guarded on either side by a stone tiger; on the lower part of the column is inscribed in English 'God is One, His is the Victory' with similar texts in Urdu, Hindi and Gurmukhi. On the wall at the back are carved the names of 4,700 Indian soldiers and labourers who died on the Western Front and have no known graves. A couple of years later, in March 1929, the 'Memorial to the Missing of the Mesopotamia Expeditionary Force' was unveiled at the Basra war cemetery in Iraq, dedicated to the memory of the British and Commonwealth war forces which included a substantial number of Indians.[4] On the Basra Memorial, 665 Indian officers are mentioned by name, but not the 33,222 other Indian ranks who are commemorated numerically.[5] Memorials were also erected in Gallipoli, Palestine and Macedonia, among other theatres. Meanwhile, throughout India and Pakistan, one comes across smaller monuments, plaques and tablets – sometimes half-known, half-remembered – to mark more local contributions: from the simple white plaque at the village of Lehri in Jhelum in Pakistan which just says 'From this village 391 men went to the Great War' and that '44 gave up

Indian troops taking part in the Victory March and Peace Pageant on 19 July 1919.

3 Stanley Rice, *Neuve-Chapelle: India's Memorial in France, 1914–18* (London, 1927).

4 This massive monument was transferred under presidential decree in 1997 to a place 32 kilometers on the road to Nasiriyah, which was part of the battleground of the Gulf War. See Philip Longworth, *The Unending Vigil: A History of the Commonwealth War Graves Commission* (London, 1988).

5 Barrett, 'Death and the Afterlife: Britain's Colonies and Dominions', 301–20.

The All India War Memorial (now known as the India Gate) serves as the national memorial to all the 70,000 soldiers of undivided India who died during 1914–1921.

6 Also see Rana Chhina, *Last Post* (Delhi, 2014). The Indian First World War memorials around the world can be found at: http://www.mea.gov.in/photo-features.htm?955.

their lives' to the Indian Cavalry Memorial at Teen Murti, Delhi to the Lascar Memorial next to the River Hoogly in Kolkata.[6]

After the war, with the passage of years, a general amnesia set in. As Europe started recovering from its wreckage, its thoughts naturally turned to its own dead, mutilated and bereaved. In India, the nationalist movement under the leadership of Mahatma Gandhi gathered force; in post-independence India, the imperial warriors were largely (but not wholly) written out of history. But amnesia is not absence. Memories of war service lingered in particular regions, communities and families – through war medals, anecdotes, songs, stories, a torn tunic, a silver coin, a diary or just a phrase [such as *l'arm*] or a tune picked up in France or Mesopotamia. Passed from generation to generation, from hand to hand or mouth to mouth, they tease us with their ineluctable blend of history and memory. A few years back, in Kolkata, I interviewed the Punjabi novelist Mohan Kahlon who lost his two uncles in Mesopotamia: his grandmother went mad with grief, the family was ruined and their village house in Lyallpur became known as 'garod' ('asylum'); war trauma thus spilled into the furthest reaches of the empire. A few months back, in Delhi, I interviewed Lieutenant-Colonel Raj Singh Gursey whose grandfather Pat Ram was also killed in the war, but the family's memories were very different. His grandfather helped in the local recruitment campaign and received silver coins and cash for his efforts; at the time of his death, his grandmother was just twenty-two and she continued to draw a war pension for another fifty-four years. She had the silver coins made into a necklace which she used to wear proudly, and the family used the cash to buy land during the partition of the country into India and Pakistan. Lieutenant-Colonel Gursey showed us a beautiful, carved walking stick and a letter, written in English, by his grandfather. Like the experience of the sepoys, there is no uniform or monolithic Indian memory of the war: it has to accommodate both these narratives.

What was the relationship between India's war service and the independence movement? Did the war hasten the process of decolonization? While it would be reductive to draw a simple, causal connection between the two, the disillusionment with the Montagu-Chelmsford reforms of 1919, the Khilafat movement and Indian nationalism in the

Twenties under the leadership of Gandhi were very much in the shadow of the war and the legitimate expectations it roused. Moreover, for the more than 900,000 men who did return, the war was an eye-opening experience: it traumatized them no doubt but it also made them more confident, more independent and more aware of their own rights. At the international level, because of its massive war contribution, India was invited to send a delegation to the Paris Peace Conference in 1919 – the team comprised the Maharajah of Kapurthala, the Bengali lawyer Sir S.P. Sinha and Lord Montagu. And it was by dint of this attendance that India was the only non-white colony to be allowed membership in the League of Nations.

Back home, it was a tale of broken promises and disillusionment, with the Amritsar massacre of 1919 happening in the very province that had contributed the highest number of men to the war effort. Feelings run so high even today that in August 2014 – as part of the war's centennial commemoration – there was a televised national debate in India: 'Was the First World War India's War? Should we remember the soldiers when they fought for the empire?'[7] Indeed, it is a fraught subject, but sixty-seven years after India's independence nationalism is perhaps not the only or most productive framework in which to examine the country's war involvement. The journey of more than one million people across the *kalo pani* to different parts of the world and serving in different theatres of war as soldiers, labourers, doctors or ambulance workers was a momentous event; mercenaries, imperial sentinels or colonial victims – or perhaps a touch of all three – these men are an essential part of the history of the country. Instead of narrow debates around whether it was 'India's war or not' or the categories of 'condemnation or celebration' – both deeply problematic – we should instead try to recover and analyze their experiences and examine the two world wars more generally in relation to India's complex, divided and contradictory histories.

In terms of cultural and literary memory, an early effort was made by the writer and nationalist Mulk Raj Anand in the form of his war novel *Across the Black Waters* (1939). Written during the Spanish Civil War and as the clouds of another world war loomed over the horizon, the novel

Marshal Foch, the Maharajah of Kapurthala and Lord Birkenhead attended the official opening of the Neuve-Chapelle (Indian) War Memorial on 7 October 1927.

7 NDTV, 'Big Fight: India and the World Wars', shown on 16 August 2014 at 8pm.

examined the Indian war experience on the Western Front in vivid and intimate detail. Anand's novel remains one of the earliest challenges to the very colour of war memory. When histories of the war had become largely white and the massive colonial contribution by around four million non-white people (Asians, Africans, West Indians and Pacific Islanders) largely sidelined, Anand powerfully reclaimed the Indian war experience: in the process, he aligned the story of a small village in the Punjab to the defining event of European history in the twentieth century.

In 2002, the Memorial Gates were inaugurated by Queen Elizabeth II in London to honour, the inscription says, 'the five million volunteers from the Indian subcontinent, Africa and the Caribbean who fought with Britain in the two World Wars'. Beside it, a small and elegant *chattri* was erected to commemorate the Indian war experience. Indeed, the Indian war experience has to be seen in relation to the experience of troops from other former colonies, not just of Britain but also of France and Germany. It also needs to be placed in relation to the Second World War, as many of these former colonies, now nation-states, struggle with these complex pasts.

As we enter the first of the five years of centennial commemoration, the accent has come to rest – firmly and irreversibly – on the middle word: First *World* War. There is a swell of interest in the South Asian war experience – from scholars, community leaders, military academies, governmental organisations, and the substantial diaspora – and a host of commemorative projects is being planned.

One of the most important and ambitious is the five-year project announced by the United Services Institution, a strategic think-tank in Delhi, which is working in collaboration with the Ministry of External Affairs: it includes a range of outputs – from international conferences and publications to wreath-laying ceremonies and commemorative missions – and is being spearheaded by the historian and retired Squadron Leader Rana T.S. Chhina.[8] In the Indian media too, there is a steady flow of articles.[9] In Great Britain, there is significant interest, from governmental initiatives – the biggest of the commemorative services held in the UK on 4 August 2014 was the one in Glasgow to remember the Commonwealth troops and was attended by Prince Charles and the prime minister – to various television and radio programmes, exhibitions and community projects.[10] Similarly across Europe – in France, Belgium, Germany, the Netherlands – conferences are being held, with public outreach events, to address the colonial war experience.

It is important to remember, in the light of these commemorative activities, that the Indian army was a multi-racial, multi-religious and multi-lingual institution, spread across India, Pakistan, Bangladesh and Burma. It is essential to recognise this ethnic, cultural and religious diversity. Moreover, a space should be created to remember the revolutionaries who fought for the subcontinent's freedom during the war years as well as for the handful of Indian deserters, conscientious objectors and the ones sentenced or shot for breach of military discipline as well as the women and chil-

8 See Rana Chinna's article 'India and the Great War', http://blogs.icrc.org/new-delhi/2014/04/11/usi-mea-world-war-i-centenary-tribute-project-to-shed-new-light-on-indias-role/.

9 See the special First World War issue of *Outlook (100 Years of War)*, 31 March 2014.

10 These include the popular exhibition *Empire, Faith and War: The Sikhs and World War One* organised by the UK Punjab Heritage Association at Brunei Gallery, SOAS, in July–September 2014.

dren who suffered. A hundred years after its outbreak, commemoration, like memory, has to be inclusive and multidirectional. At the same time, a space should also be made available for reflection and critique rather than simple remembrance. Often, particular sanitised views of the past are promoted to fit the multicultural present of modern-day Europe. While Indian soldiers came to fight in Europe and there were pockets of intimacy and affection between individual sepoys and British and European men and women, many of the imperial ideologies and racist institutional structures were unfortunately in place. And we cannot afford to forget these painful and unattractive aspects. There is often an impulse today to retrospectively turn these colonial soldiers into 'heroes' and 'martyrs', even though many enlisted to keep debtors at bay and had a conflicted relationship to their job. Colonial war commemoration sometimes slips into 'celebration'. But these are histories of trauma and bloodshed. While it is essential to challenge the colour of war memory, it is also important to keep a careful watch on the way it is being done: there is much to commemorate, recover and understand, little to 'celebrate'.

In 1918, a few months before his death in November, the British poet Wilfred Owen – the most popular name associated with the First World War – was reading Rabindranath Tagore's Nobel-prize-winning anthology *Gitanjali*. As he left home for the final time, Owen's last words to his dear mother were a line from Tagore: 'When I go from hence, let this be my parting word/That what I have seen is unsurpassable.' The subjects of this book – Tagore's fellow-countrymen and colonial brethren – could not have agreed more as they came to Europe not just to see but to take part in the 'unsurpassable' – both in terms of wonder and horror. This book takes one particular source – photographs – and one particular theatre of war – the Western Front – to delve into the area. Hopefully, it will be a spur for further investigation of the topic as well as of other important Indian theatres of the war such as Mesopotamia (India's main battleground), Gallipoli, Egypt, Palestine and East Africa.

The Neuve-Chapelle War Memorial with its white circular boundary wall with the *chattris* and the tall column in the middle and a carved stone tiger on either side.

Table of illustrations

Acronyms and abbreviations
IWM: Imperial War Museum
SHD: Service Historique de la Défense, SHD fonds Rumpf
BDIC: Bibliothèque de Documentation Internationale Contemporaine
t: top
a: above
m: middle
b: bottom/below
l: left
r: right

The 'fonds Rumpf' (SHD/GR, 2 K 247) is a special collection that is held in the pictorial archives division of the Service Historique de la Défense in Vincennes. Although it bears the name of its donor, it is in fact a photographic archive assembled by Victor Forbin (1864–1947). Forbin was a great traveller, journalist, well-known author and scientific populariser. He contributed to various magazines, including *Le Petit Journal* and *L'Illustration*. To enliven his writings, he acquired photographs from press agencies and military and civil bodies but also from private collectors. He also made money out of it by acting as a photographic correspondent for British and American press organs. The collection that he built up is unique and consists of 50,286 prints and 3,374 glass plates and flexible negatives.

Jacket image
P. 95: 'War-time Bastille Day'. Photograph published in the magazine *Excelsior*, Saturday 15 July 1916. © Wackernie/Excelsio-L'Equipe/Roger-Viollet.

Introduction India, Europe and the First World War
9 'The Empire Needs Men!' © Mary Evans Picture Library/Onslow Auctions Limited/Rue des Archives
10 t Map of British India, Waterlow & Sons (London), 1930. Département Cartes et Plans, Bibliothèque Nationale de France, GE D-9961 © BnF
10 m Memorabilia of Captain Dr Manindranath Das. Private collection, India
10 b *Lota*. Collection Dominique Faivre
11 Charity collection in aid of the Indian troops. SHD/fonds Rumpf, Vincennes
12 Letter and envelope from an Indian soldier on the Western Front. Haryana Academy of History and Culture, India
13 Distribution of quinine to the Indian troops in Africa. SHD/fonds Rumpf, Vincennes
14 Indian troops disembarking in Mesopotamia. SHD/fonds Rumpf, Vincennes
15 Indian soldiers engage in mule-back wrestling, Salonika, 1916. SHD/fonds Rumpf, Vincennes
17 'Indian War Loan 1918'. Poster by J.L. Herbert Dobson, IWM, London © IWM

Chapter 1 The home front
20 Officers bidding farewell to Indian troops, Bombay, August 1914. IWM, London © IWM
22 l 'Who Will Take this Uniform, Money and Rifle?', recruitment poster, text in Urdu. Printed by Saleem Press, Lahore. IWM, London © IWM
22 r 'The Best Support is Supporting the Government', poster, text in Urdu. Published by the Punjab War Loan Committee. IWM, London © IWM
23 'The Gurkhas', French postcard. SHD/fonds Michat, Vincennes
24 Simla, the summer capital of British India. SHD/fonds Rumpf, Vincennes
25 Clock-tower, Chandni Chowk, Delhi. SHD/fonds Rumpf, Vincennes
26 Calcutta at night, SHD/fonds Rumpf, Vincennes
27 Horses resting in Bombay. IWM, London © IWM
27 b Karachi harbour, postcard. Private collection, Paris
28 a The *jirga* at Dardoni with the Wazir *maliks* listening to the peace terms. SHD/fonds Rumpf, Vincennes
28 b A view of the encampment of the 54th Sikhs. SHD/fonds Rumpf, Vincennes
29 A loyal British outpost on the Afghan frontier. SHD/fonds Rumpf, Vincennes
30 Bombardment of Madras by the SMS *Emden*. SHD/fonds Rumpf, Vincennes
31 Bombardment of Madras by the *Emden*: damage done to the Pantheon Club. SHD/fonds Rumpf, Vincennes
32 a Procession of Indian cavalry, Bangalore. SHD/fonds Rumpf, Vincennes
32 b Party of recruits for the 2nd Lancers. IWM, London
33 Sepoys wearing European uniform. SHD/fonds Rumpf, Vincennes
34 t 'Our Day' ladies, 19 October 1916, London © Topical Press Agency/Getty Images
34–5 A recruiting meeting being held at one of the hill fairs, 12/10 1917. IWM, London © IWM
36 A non-literate Indian soldier acknowledging receipt of pay by a thumb-impression. SHD/fonds Rumpf, Vincennes
37 a Swearing-in of infantry recruits, Benares. IWM, London © IWM
37 b Indian troops at physical training. IWM, London © IWM
38–9 Home rule for India, 1917. IWM, London © IWM
40–1 Transport carts at Bombay docks. IWM, London © IWM
42 An Indian unit on a transport ship. IWM, London © IWM
43 Indians at drill on the deck of a transport ship. SHD/fonds Michat, Vincennes

Chapter 2 To the front
44 The troops parading on their arrival in Marseilles, September 1914. SHD/fonds Michat, Vincennes
46 l Indian lancer serving under General Johnson, Béthune, 16 December 1914. Drawing by Paul Sarrut © The British Library
46 r and 47 l Burnand portraits. From Eugène Burnand, *Les Alliés dans la guerre des nations* (1922)
47 r Unloading the Indian troops' equipment. SHD/fonds Rumpf, Vincennes
48–9 The arrival of the Indian troops in France. SHD/fonds Rumpf, Vincennes
50–1 The Indian army's camp at Parc Borély, Marseilles. Postcards. Imprimerie Provençale-Guéraud-Marseille. SHD/fonds Michat, Vincennes
52 l Hindu troops. Postcard. Éditions Historiques de l'Ancienne Photographie Provost à Toulouse, Paris. SHD/fonds Michat, Vincennes
52 r Convoy heading towards Toulouse:. Éditions Historiques de l'Ancienne Photographie Provost à Toulouse, Paris. SHD/fonds Michat, Vincennes
53 Indian cavalry on the march: official photograph taken on the front in France. SHD/fonds Rumpf, Vincennes
54 Indian troops in Orléans, 1914 © Maurice-Louis Branger/Roger-Viollet
55 t In the Indians' camp. Postcard. SHD/fonds Michat, Vincennes
55 b British Indian army passing in front of the statue of Joan of Arc, Orléans, 1914. Postcard. SHD/fonds Michat, Vincennes
56–7 Indian soldiers in transit, 1915 © Maurice-Louis Branger/Roger-Viollet
58 Hindu soldiers preparing their meal at Le Landy station in Saint-Denis on the outskirts of Paris, October 1914. BDIC/Fonds Valois, Paris
59 Indian soldiers cooking chapattis at the Gare du Nord, Paris, 1914 © Maurice-Louis Branger/Roger-Viollet

Chapter 3 The front and beyond
60 Two Indian soldiers stationed at Neuve-Chapelle, March 1915. SHD/fonds Rumpf, Vincennes
62 l The first Indian to win the Victoria Cross. Photo published in the *Daily Mirror*, London, January 1915
62 r Sir D. Haig introducing Pertab Singh to General Joffre. Postcard. SHD/fonds Michat, Vincennes
63 l Map of the Battle of Neuve-Chapelle, 10–12 March 1915 © In Flanders Fields Museum, Ypres
63 r Sikhs in a devastated forest. Illustration by Alberto Fabio Lorenzi © BDIC-Musée de l'Histoire Contemporaine, Paris
64 Allied Indian troops arriving on the front, France © Herbert/Archive Photos/Getty Images
65 Second line of Gurkhas. Collection Eric Deroo, Paris. Photo © Frédéric Hanoteau/Éditions Gallimard
66 Gurkhas digging communication trenches. Stereoscopic view by H.D. Girdwood. Collection Eric Deroo, Paris. Photo © Frédéric Hanoteau/Éditions Gallimard
67 Infantry in the front-line trenches preparing to meet a gas attack. Collection Eric Deroo, Paris. Photo © Frédéric Hanoteau/Éditions Gallimard
68 Officers seek refuge when shellfire becomes too dangerous, Paris. Photo © Frédéric Hanoteau/Éditions Gallimard 69 Company of the Black Watch. Collection Eric Deroo, Paris. Photo © Frédéric Hanoteau/Éditions Gallimard
70 a–70 b Sepoys behind the front line. SHD/fonds Rumpf, Vincennes
71 A wounded Indian, 1915. BDIC/Fonds Valois, Paris
72 VCOs (Viceroy's Commissioned Officers) and other ranks of the 57th Wilde's Rifles take aim in the trenches on the outskirts of Wytschaete, Belgium. Photo by Paul-Lucien Maze. IWM, London © IWM
73 Indian soldiers of the Army Cycle Corps during the Battle of the Somme, July 1916. IWM, London © IWM
74–5 A detachment of cavalry of the British Indian army on the northern front © Maurice-Louis Branger/Roger-Viollet
76 and 77 Hindu troops stop on the road from Villers-Cotterêts to Soissons, 21 July 1918. BDIC/fonds Valois, Paris
78 The quarters of Indian soldiers employed at the British airfield, Gerbéviller, 1917. BDIC, Paris/fonds Valois
79 Group of Sikhs. Photo by Jean Segaud. Musée de l'Armée, Paris. Photo © Musée de l'Armée, Dist. RMN-GP/image musée de l'Armée
80 Group of Sikh soldiers, Paris. Photo © Musée de l'Armée, Dist. RMN-GP/Pascal Segrette
81 Group of armed Gurkhas. Photo by Jean Segaud. Musée de l'Armée, Paris. Photo © Musée de l'Armée, Dist. RMN-GP/Pascal Segrette
82 Indian attending to his ablutions. Photo by Jean Segaud. Musée de l'Armée, Paris. Photo © Musée de l'Armée, Dist. RMN-GP/image musée de l'Armée
83 Indian with his hair down after performing his ablutions. Photo by Jean Segaud, Musée de l'Armée, Paris. Photo © Musée de l'Armée, Dist. RMN-GP/image musée de l'Armée
84 t *Dhobi* or Indian washerman hanging out the laundry. SHD/fonds Rumpf, Vincennes
84 b Indian barber, Neuve-Chapelle. SHD/fonds Rumpf, Vincennes
85 Indian barber cutting a soldier's moustache. SHD/fonds Rumpf, Vincennes
86 t An improvised oven in the Orléans camp, November 1914 © Caudrilliers/Excelsior-L'Equipe/Roger-Viollet
86 b Indian cooks preparing a native dish for Indian troops. SHD/fonds Rumpf, Vincennes
87 Indian eating chapattis, Paris. SHD/fonds Rumpf, Vincennes
88 Slaughter of goats for our Indian troops, in accordance with sacred rites. Collection Eric Deroo, Paris. Photo © Frédéric Hanoteau/Éditions Gallimard
89 Indian cook at the Azelot camp, 1918. BDIC, Paris/fonds Valois
90 t Bastille Day Parade, 14 July 1916: the Indian infantry marching down the Avenue Alexandre III. BDIC, Paris/fonds Valois
90 b Bastille Day Parade, 14 July 1916: review of the Allied (Indian) troops on the Champs-Élysées. BDIC, Paris/fonds Valois
91 Bastille Day Parade on the Champs-Élysées. Collection Eric Deroo, Paris. Photo © Frédéric Hanoteau/Éditions Gallimard

92 'War-time Bastille Day'. Photograph published in the magazine *Excelsior*, Saturday 15 July 1916 © Wackernie/Excelsior-L'Equipe/Roger-Viollet
93 Bastille Day Parade in Paris. Indian soldiers on Place de la Concorde, Paris © Wackernie/Excelsior-L'Equipe/Roger-Viollet
94 l Soldiers of the British Indian army, France, c 1915 © The Print Collector/Getty Images
94 r A little French girl welcomes the Hindu soldiers. Postcard, SHD/fonds Michat, Vincennes
95 Soldier of the British Indian army, France, c 1915 © The Print Collector/Getty Images
96 Two Indian soldiers billeted at a farm in northern France. Collection Eric Deroo, Paris. Photo © Frédéric Hanoteau/Éditions Gallimard
97 Sikhs and French villagers © British Library, London/Leemage
98 A field post office. Collection Eric Deroo, Paris. Photo © Frédéric Hanoteau/Éditions Gallimard
99 t Hindu soldiers sorting the mail. SHD/fonds Rumpf, Vincennes
99 b Members of an Indian labour battalion reading papers during a work break, 1917 © Illustrated London News/Mary Evans/Rue des Archives
100 Sikhs singing religious chants in a French barn © British Library, London/Leemage
101 Indian troops during the Muslim festival, c 1916 © FPG/Hulton Archive/Getty Images
102 t and b 'The Indian mules' dust bath'. SHD/fonds Rumpf, Vincennes
103 In a Sikhs' camp. SHD/fonds Rumpf, Vincennes
104 British airfield, Azelot, 12 February 1918: Hindus going to work. BDIC, Paris/fonds Valois
105 British airfield, Azelot, 12 February 1918: Hindus chopping wood. BDIC Paris/fonds Valois
106 t British airfield, Azelot, 12 February 1918: Hindus digging a drainage trench. BDIC, Paris/fonds Valois
106 b and 107 British airfield, Azelot, 12 February 1918: Hindus employed in the felling of trees. BDIC, Paris/fonds Valois
108 Sir Pertab Singh in Montreuil-sur-Mer. SHD/fonds Rumpf, Vincennes
109 The Maharajah of Patiala. SHD/fonds Rumpf, Vincennes

Chapter 4 Hospitals
110 The Brighton Dome © The Print Collector/Getty Images
112 The Dome during its use as a military hospital. Watercolour painting by Douglas Fox-Pitt, 1915. Royal Pavilion & Museums, Brighton & Hove. Released for re-use under a BY-NC-SA 4.0 Creative Commons licence
113 l *Brighton and Hove and South Sussex Graphic*, Saturday 13 February 1915 © Royal Pavilion & Museums, Brighton & Hove
113 r Indian Red Cross workers having a rest behind the firing line. SHD/fonds Rumpf, Vincennes
114 Arrival of casualties. Collection Eric Deroo, Paris. Photo © Frédéric Hanoteau/Éditions Gallimard
115 l Stretchers-bearers lifting a serious case. Collection Eric Deroo, Paris. Photo © Frédéric Hanoteau/Éditions Gallimard
115 r Ambulances waiting to receive casualties. Collection Eric Deroo, Paris. Photo © Frédéric Hanoteau/Éditions Gallimard
116 The military school converted into an Indian hospital,, Musée de France Roger Rodière, Montreuil-sur-Mer
117 Convalescent Indian soldiers. Collection J. Demont
118 t Convalescent soldiers. Photo by A.H. Fry. Royal Pavilion and Museums, Brighton & Hove
118 b Wounded listening to the bag pipe and sunning themselves © British Library, London/Leemage
119 A wounded soldier dictating a letter to a sepoy IWM, London © IWM
120 Indian soldiers in beds in their room at the Pavilion Hospital, 1915. Royal Pavilion and Museums, Brighton & Hove
121 Wounded Indians at the Corn Exchange, Brighton. Royal Pavilion and Museums, Brighton & Hove
122 t The X-ray room at the Kitchener Hospital, Brighton © British Library, London/Leemage
122 b Electrical and galvanic treatment room at the Kitchener Hospital, Brighton. © British Library, London/Leemage
123 Wounded native officers at the Kitchener Hospital, Brighton. British Library, London/Leemage
124 Indian convalescents. Hampshire County Council
125 t Indian soldiers who were wounded fighting in Flanders recuperating at Bournemouth, c 1917 © Underwood Archives/Getty Images
125 b Mont Dore Hospital, Bournemouth. Stereoscopic view by H.D. Girdwood © British Library, London/Leemage
126 t Convalescent Indian soldiers enjoy a performance at the Lady Hardinge Hospital, Brockenhurst, Hampshire. SHD/fonds Rumpf, Vincennes
126 b In front of the hut. SHD/fonds Rumpf, Vincennes
127 Miss Gakarjan talks to wounded warriors. SHD/fonds Rumpf, Vincenness

Chapter 5 Prisoners
128 In the Wünsdorf camp,. Photo by Otto Stiehl. Museum Europäischer Kulturen, Berlin © BPK, Berlin, Dist. RMN-GP/image BPK
130 l Otto Stiehl, cover page of the book *Unsere Feinde: 96 Charakterköpfe aus deutschen Kriegsgefangenenlagern* (Stuttgart, 1916). Collection Eric Deroo, Paris. Photo © Frédéric Hanoteau/Éditions Gallimard
130 r Portraits of Indian prisoners, by Hermann Struck. From *Prisoners of War: 100 Lithographs by Hermann Struck*, with a preface by Prof. Dr F. von Luschan (Berlin, 1916) 131 'Garfwoti'. Museum Europäischer Kulturen, Berlin © BPK, Berlin, Dist. RMN-GP/image BPK
131 r Portrait of two Gurkhas. From *Deutschlands Gegner im Weltkriege* (Berlin, 1925). Collection Eric Deroo, Paris. Photo © Frédéric Hanoteau/Éditions Gallimard
132 Group of English and Indian prisoners. Collection Eric Deroo Paris. Photo © Frédéric Hanoteau/Éditions Gallimard
133 t Group portrait of prisoners: British, French, Russian and Indian men at Friedrichsfeld camp, 1915. IWM, London
133 b Two Gurkhas photographed at the Schneidemühl camp. IWM, London © IWM
134–5 The Wünsdorf camp and the mosque © BPK, Berlin, Dist. RMN-GP/image BPK
136 Group of prisoners, Wünsdorf. Collection Eric Deroo, Paris. Photo © Frédéric Hanoteau,' Éditions Gallimard
137 The detainees of the so-called Halfmoon Camp, c. 1915. Photo © BPK, Berlin, Dist. RMN-GP/image BPK
138–9 Spring festival: show performed by Indian prisoners at Wünsdorf. Photo by Otto Stiehl. © BPK, Berlin, Dist. RMN-GP/image BPK
140 t An audio-recording session taking place at the Halfmoon Camp, Wünsdorf. From Otto Stiehl, *Unsere Feinde* (Stuttgart, 1916)
140 b A study on the Gurung language with the prisoners of the Wünsdorf camp. Lüders Archive, Berlin/*Unsere Feinde* (Stuttgart, 1916)
141 Portrait of Sultan Singh, Rajput, Wünsdorf camp. Photo by Otto Stiehl. Museum Europäischer Kulturen © BPK, Berlin, Dist. RMN-GP/image BPK
142 Portrait of a Gurkha prisoner: Serg. Ganga Ram of Dharmsala. Photo by Otto Stiehl. Museum Europäischer Kulturen © BPK, Berlin, Dist. RMN-GP/image BPK
143 Indian prisoners at the Wünsdorf camp. Collection Eric Deroo, Paris. Photo © Frédéric Hanoteau/Éditions Gallimard

Afterword
145 Indian troops participating in the Victory March, London. SHD/fonds Rumpf, Vincennes
146 The All India War Memorial (today the India Gate), Delhi. Postcard. Private collection, Paris
147 Unveiling of the Hindu Memorial in Neuve-Chapelle (Pas-de-Calais). Collection Archives Départementales du Nord, Lille/Fonds Scrive, 39 Fl 153
149 Monument at Neuve-Chapelle. Postcard. Private collection, Paris

Mission du centenaire de la Première Guerre mondiale
(First World War Centenary Partnership Program)

Created in 2012, the First World War Centenary Partnership Program (Mission du centenaire de la Première Guerre Mondiale) was tasked by the French government with planning and implementing the First World War centenary programme. It is responsible for organising the major commemorative events, supporting and co-ordinating initiatives that are being launched all over France and keeping the general public informed about Centenary preparations and programming. With the help of a dynamic nationwide network, since 2013 the Centenary Partnership Program has initiated more than 3,000 projects, 2,000 of which have been awarded the official 'Centenaire' seal. This seal recognises the most innovative projects and makes them eligible for financing from the Centenary Fund, the initiative fund created by the Program to support the Centenary initiatives. The 'Centenaire' seal is mainly applied to activities carried out on home soil, but also promotes activities organised abroad, especially in countries that were enemies of France during the First World War.

Centenaire.org: a digital space devoted to the centenary of the First World War

Centenaire.org is the Centenary Partnership Program digital resources portal. It allows the general public, those interested in issues of memory, history lovers and teachers to discover, experience and understand this major memorial event. The site includes a national and international gateway devoted to Centenary events and to memory tourism. It offers numerous excerpts from private and public archives complete with commentaries, files on contemporary cultural themes and a calendar listing all the exhibitions, activities and events linked to the Centenary. It also provides an educational area for teachers and an academic area devoted to publications by experts on the First World War.
www.centenaire.org

The DMPA's missions

The Directorate of Memory, Heritage and Archives (Direction de la Mémoire, du Patrimoine et des Archives or DMPA) is a directorate of the French Ministry of Defence, acting under the authority of the ministry's general secretary. The DMPA has particular responsibility for the ministry's cultural policy through the collections of its museums, archive services and libraries. It decides on and funds the necessary action to manage and promote this rich legacy. It is in this context that the DMPA also pursues a policy of publishing and supporting the production of books and audio-visual materials, allowing a wide public to discover the history and heritage of the Ministry of Defence.

The SHD

The Defence Historical Service (Service Historique de la Défense or SHD) is the Ministry of Defence's archives centre and also includes a specialist library that is one of the best stocked in France. The service is responsible for accrediting, cataloguing and gathering items of military symbolism and contributing to publications relating to the history of conflicts, armies and defence. A first-rate documentary resource, its collections (380 linear kilometres of archives dating back to the seventeenth century, with 600,000 volumes) represent an important part of the nation's memory – one that the SHD's archivists, librarians, historians and technicians work hard to preserve, transmit and share.

Acknowledgments

The author is grateful to Elisabeth de Farcy for asking him to do the book and to Elizabeth Robertson for her invaluable assistance with its various aspects: their constant enthusiasm and help made the book possible. He would also like to warmly thank Geneviève de la Bretesche, Vincent Lever and Sarah Kane for their painstaking editorial work and wonderful attention to detail, and to Rana Chhina, Manuele Destors (at Gallimard) and Hugh Stevens for their general support.

For the trust that they have placed in us for several years, the publishers would like to thank the Ministry of Defence and the departments within it devoted to the nation's heritage:
- at the DMPA, Philippe Navelot, Laurent Veyssière, Isabelle Solano and Mathilde Meyer;
- at the SHD, in Vincennes, Odile Jurbert, Benjamin Doizelet and Sylvie Yeomans.

The publishers would also like to express their gratitude to the following for their assistance and co-operation:
- Cyril Burté at the BDIC, Helen Mavin at the Imperial War Museum, Jean-François Graillot at the Musée-Citadelle in Montreuil-sur-Mer, Dr J. Demont in Montreuil-sur-Mer, and, in particular, Éric Deroo, for his inexhaustible collections.
- His Excellency Arun K. Singh, the Indian ambassador in Paris, who has been enormously supportive of exhibitions and publications commemorating the Indian presence in France.
- In Delhi, (Retd) Squadron Leader Rana Chhina, in charge of the 'India and the Great War' commemorations, Max Claudet, counsellor for culture at the French embassy and Judith Oriol, literary attaché.

Finally, this book owes its publication to the enthusiasm and the support of Joseph Zimet, general director of the Mission du centenaire de la Première Guerre Mondiale (along with MBDA who is taking an active interest in the Centenary Programme).